SCIENCE ENCYCLOPEDIAS

THE SPACE ENCYCLOPEDIA

BY GAIL RADLEY

Abdo Reference

An Imprint of Abdo Publishing
abdobooks.com

TABLE OF CONTENTS

INTRODUCTION **4**

THE SUN **8**
    The Active Sun 12
    Birth and Death of the Sun 16
    The Sun and Life 20
    Studying the Sun 26
    Light Shows 28

PLANETS **32**
    Mercury 36
    Venus 38
    Earth 40
    Mars 42
    Jupiter 44
    Saturn 46
    Uranus 48
    Neptune 50
    Dwarf Planets 52
    Exoplanets 56

THE MOON **58**
    What the Moon Is Made Of 60
    Birth of the Moon 64
    Moon Phases 66
    The Moon's Effects on Earth 70

SPACE EXPLORATION **78**
    The Space Race 82
    Exploring the Solar System 88
    Space Stations 96
    Shuttling into Space 102
    Space Tourism 108

**ASTEROIDS, COMETS, AND
METEOROIDS** **112**
    The Solar System's Leftovers 114
    When Meteorites Land 118
    Fear of Falling Objects 122
    Famous Asteroids and Comets 126

STARS **132**
   A Star Is Born.. 134
   Stars of Many Colors 136
   Constellations... 144
   Notable Stars 148

GALAXIES **150**
   The Early Galaxy 152
   The Size and Shape of
      the Milky Way 156
   Galaxy Diversity 160
   Discovering More Galaxies 164
   The Andromeda Collision 168
   Galaxy Clusters... 170

THE UNIVERSE **172**
   The Big Bang... 174
   The Observable Universe 176
   Dark Energy and Dark Matter 178
   The Multiverse?... 184

CONCLUSION................................... **186**

GLOSSARY **188**

TO LEARN MORE................................ **189**

INDEX **190**

PHOTO CREDITS **191**

INTRODUCTION

For thousands of years, human cultures have had a deep interest in the skies above them. The motions of objects in the sky told the people of North America many things. These things included when to plant, when to harvest, when to hunt, and when to celebrate. Researchers think England's Stonehenge structure was a temple designed to follow the sun's movements. In Africa, a stone circle built 7,000 years ago tracked the summer solstice and the arrival of the rainy season. Many cultures saw gods and goddesses, moral lessons, and hints of things to come in the night sky. As humans learned

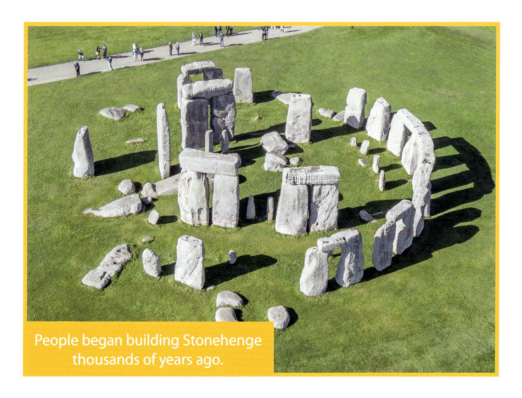

People began building Stonehenge thousands of years ago.

In this diagram, the blue line represents the Kármán line. The red line shows the altitude of a space station about 250 miles (400 km) above the surface.

more about the natural world, they began to discover the scientific nature of the things they saw in the sky.

There is no distinct boundary above Earth where space begins. The atmosphere gradually becomes thinner and thinner as the altitude increases. But one commonly accepted point for this transition is the Kármán line. Named for scientist Theodore von Kármán, it is located at an altitude of 62 miles (100 km) above the planet's surface.

INTRODUCTION

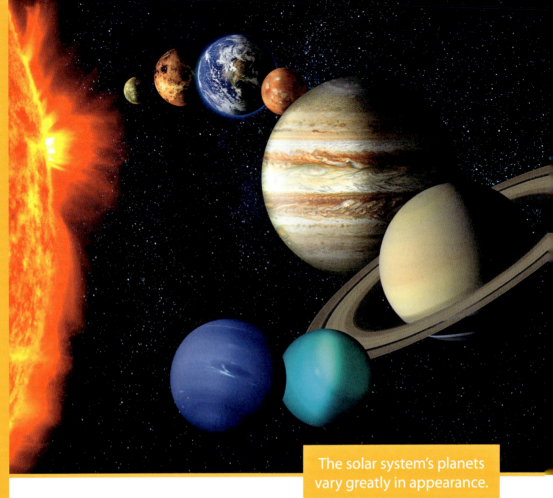

The solar system's planets vary greatly in appearance.

TRAVELING OUTWARD

Earth's nearest neighbor in space is the moon. It is the only natural object orbiting Earth. Earth is the third of eight planets orbiting the sun. Several of these planets have their own moons. Smaller objects such as asteroids and comets also orbit the sun. The sun, planets, moons, and other objects all make up the solar system.

Discussing distances in space can be difficult because the distances are so large. One useful tool is the speed of light. Light always moves at the same speed. Saying how long it takes light to travel from place to place is a simple way to give distances. For example, the moon is about 1.3 light-seconds from Earth. In other words, it takes 1.3 seconds for a beam of light to make that trip. Light takes about four hours to go from the sun to Neptune, the most distant planet in our solar system.

The sun is one of about 100 billion stars in the Milky Way galaxy. These stars are very far apart. The nearest star to our sun is called Proxima Centauri. It is about 4.25 light-years away.

The Milky Way is not the only galaxy. There are at least 100 billion other galaxies in space. The nearest is the Canis Major Dwarf galaxy. It is about 25,000 light-years away. Together, all the galaxies make up the known universe.

Over time, scientists have learned a great deal about space. Spacecraft and telescopes have unlocked many secrets of galaxies, stars, planets, and more. But with such a vast frontier in the night sky, there is still much more to discover.

With telescopes, scientists have learned a lot about the universe around us.

THE SUN

For much of human history, many people believed Earth was fixed in the center of space. They thought the other planets and the sun revolved around it. This concept is now known as the geocentric model. Thinkers such as the Greek scholar Ptolemy, who worked in the 100s CE, were strong supporters of this idea.

Early thinkers believed Earth was at the center of the universe.

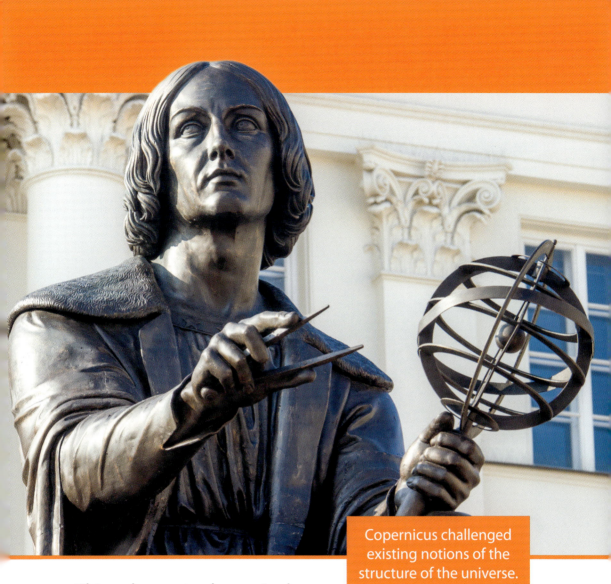

Copernicus challenged existing notions of the structure of the universe.

    Things began to change in the 1500s. The Polish scholar Nicolaus Copernicus proposed the idea that the sun was at the center, and Earth was simply one of several planets revolving around it. This concept is the heliocentric model. It came into conflict with some religious teachings relating to the nature of the sun and Earth. For decades after Copernicus published his idea, it was not widely accepted.

THE SUN

The Italian astronomer Galileo Galilei revisited the idea in the early 1600s. The concept of heliocentrism soon reached a much broader audience. Religious authorities banned Galileo's book and punished him. But new observations by Galileo and other scientists provided more evidence for the heliocentric model. By the mid-1600s, most astronomers supported this idea.

Artwork depicts the trial of Galileo for supporting concepts that went against religious authorities.

Centuries after his death, Galileo was honored with the naming of the *Galileo* probe, which explored Jupiter.

THE SUN

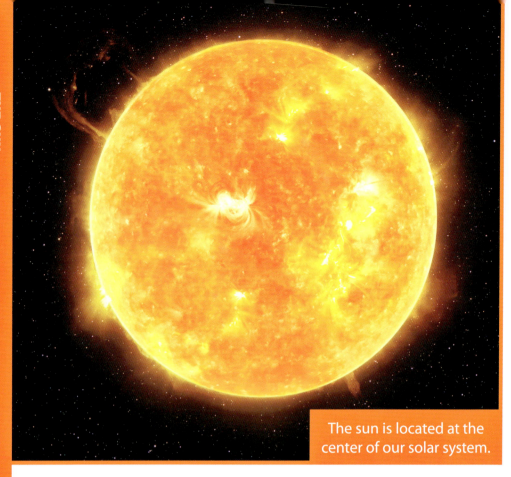

The sun is located at the center of our solar system.

THE ACTIVE SUN

At dawn, the planets seem to disappear, and stars no longer seem to twinkle above. But one great, glowing star remains: the sun. It is the only star in our solar system, and it is located about 93 million miles (150 million km) from Earth. The sun generates energy by fusing atoms of one element, hydrogen, together to form atoms of another element, helium. The fusion process releases enormous amounts of heat. The sun's core reaches temperatures of 27 million degrees Fahrenheit (15 million°C). Energy is released from the sun in all directions as light. When that light strikes the objects of the solar system, including Earth, it warms them.

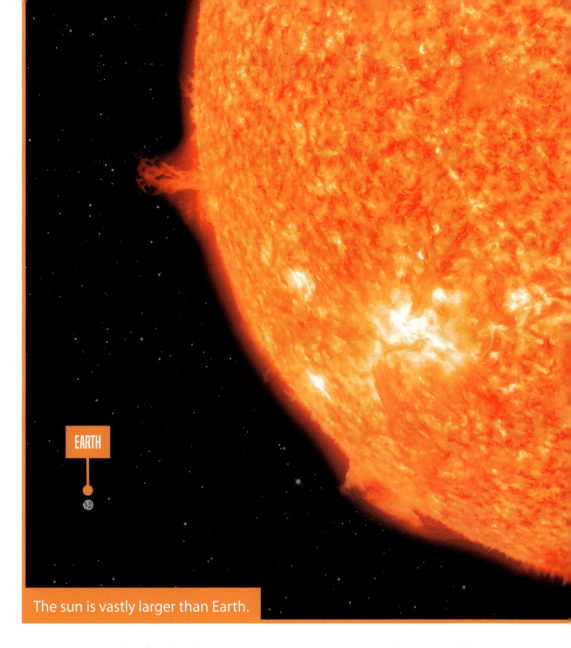

The sun is vastly larger than Earth.

The sun is by far the largest and most massive object in the solar system. Its diameter is about 109 times the diameter of Earth. If it were an empty container, it could hold more than one million Earths. The sun makes up an incredible 99.8 percent of the solar system's mass. The planets, moons, asteroids, and comets make up the remaining 0.2 percent.

THE SUN

Still, as stars go, the sun is about average. Other stars range from one-tenth the sun's width to 100 times wider. The sun is a type of star known as a yellow dwarf star. Its light, while technically white, turns yellow when seen through Earth's atmosphere.

From Earth, sunlight usually looks yellow.

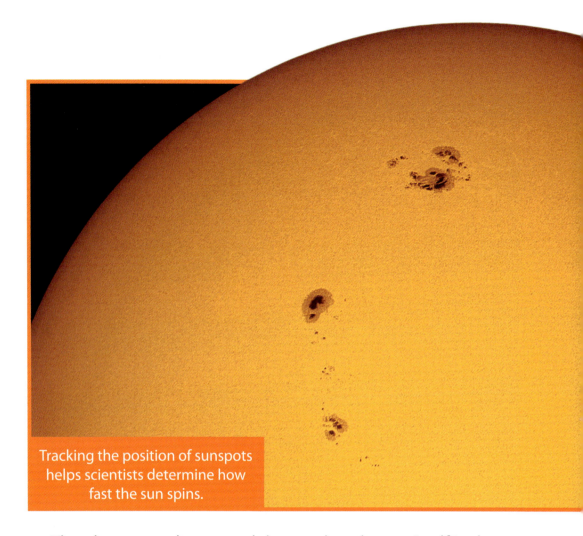

Tracking the position of sunspots helps scientists determine how fast the sun spins.

    The planets revolve around the sun, but the sun itself is also in motion. Like the planets, it rotates on its axis. Scientists track the sun's rotation by looking at the movement of its sunspots, which are dark spots on the sun's surface. Because the sun is made up of burning gas rather than solid matter, some parts rotate faster and some more slowly. It takes 25 days for the sun's middle, or equator, to make one full rotation. At the sun's poles, it takes about 36 days. At the same time, the sun is orbiting the center of the galaxy. One trip around the galactic core takes about 230 million years.

THE SUN

Stars are born in gigantic clouds of dust and gas called nebulae.

BIRTH AND DEATH OF THE SUN

Scientists believe that the sun formed about 4.6 billion years ago out of the solar nebula, a spinning cloud of dust and gases. Something caused the nebula to collapse. It may have been shock waves from an exploding star, called a supernova. It may have collapsed from the pull of its own gravity. Whatever happened, the nebula was compressed into a disk. Most of the disk was pulled into the center. Heat and pressure built up as more and more gas was compressed in the center. Eventually the fusion process began, and hydrogen started turning into helium. It took about 50 million years from the start of the collapse until the sun was fully formed.

Once enough gas is compressed for fusion to begin, a star is born.

THE SUN

The sun has a limited amount of hydrogen fuel. Scientists believe it will start to run out in about five billion years. Once that happens, the core will begin collapsing, forcing the sun's outer layers closer to the center and increasing the star's temperature. With hydrogen still in the outer layers, the sun will continue to produce energy for a while. The outer layers will swell, turning the sun into what is known as a red giant. It will grow so large that it will swallow the inner planets, including Earth.

Scientists believe that billions of years from now, the sun will dramatically increase in size.

A star in the white dwarf part of its life cycle is far smaller and dimmer than it once was.

When all the outer layers burn away, only the star's core will be left. At this point, it will shrink down to become what scientists call a white dwarf. It will be small but still extremely hot. As it cools, its light will fade out. Scientists believe that many billions of years later, the sun will eventually become completely dark.

Sunlight is vital for plant life to grow and thrive.

THE SUN AND LIFE

The sun's energy makes life on Earth possible. Plants rely on a process called photosynthesis. They use the sun's light to convert carbon dioxide and water into glucose and oxygen. Glucose, a form of sugar, provides plants with energy to grow. People and animals can then eat the growing plants for food. Photosynthesis turns light energy into chemical energy. The other product, oxygen, goes into the atmosphere. Animals need to breathe oxygen to survive. Almost all of Earth's living things rely on the sun in some way.

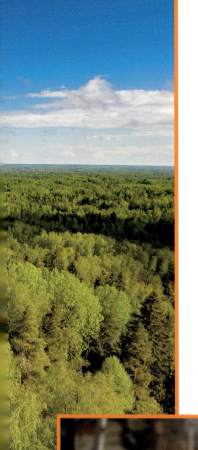

The sun keeps people healthy in other ways than by helping to provide food and oxygen. Sunlight causes the skin to produce vitamin D, which is needed for strong bones and protection from illness. Sunlight also helps control body levels of the hormones melatonin and serotonin. Melatonin helps a person get good sleep. Serotonin improves mood. Some people who are deprived of regular sunshine may feel depressed due to a lack of serotonin.

Moderate exposure to sunlight has important health benefits.

THE SUN

People have long harnessed the sun's energy for a variety of uses. Ancient people from Rome to North America positioned their houses to take advantage of the sun's warmth. In the 1700s, a Swiss scientist built a solar oven. This box trapped the sun's heat to cook food.

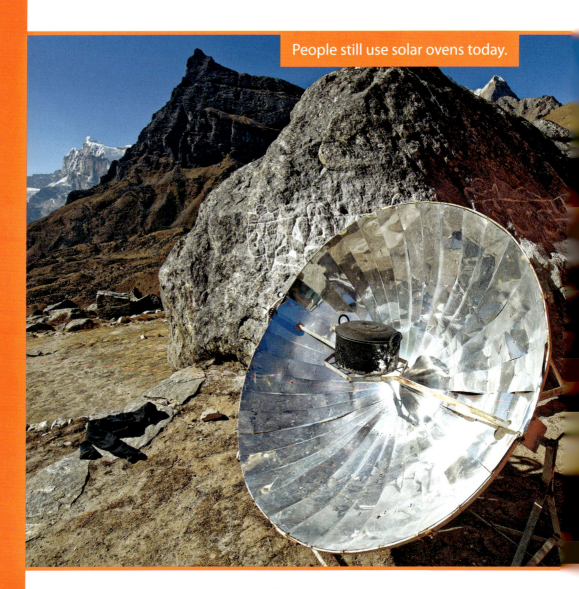

People still use solar ovens today.

Some early solar cells were used to power spacecraft.

In the 1800s, scientists noticed that light could produce small electric currents. They wondered if they could turn solar energy directly into usable electricity. American inventor Charles Fritts created a device to do this in 1883, but it generated very little power. In 1954, scientists at Bell Labs in the United States invented the first practical solar cell. In a demonstration, they showed it could power a small toy.

THE SUN

Large fields of solar panels generate significant amounts of electricity.

Since then, solar panels have become larger, cheaper, and more efficient. They are a major source of renewable energy today. Many people put them on the roofs of their homes. Power companies build vast fields of panels. As long as the sun is shining, these panels can create electricity without producing pollution.

As much good as the sun does for people, it can also create problems. Too much sun exposure can put people's health at risk. It can cause painful burns known as sunburns, which also increase a person's risk for skin cancer. Eyes can suffer sunburn as well, leading to vision problems. Solar flares, which are huge explosions on the sun, can send particles out into space. When they hit Earth, these particles can cause electrical storms that knock out power systems and damage communication satellites.

Wearing hats and applying sunscreen protects against the harmful effects of sunlight.

The *Parker Solar Probe* went through intense testing before launch.

STUDYING THE SUN

Due to the sun's intense heat, sending a spacecraft to study it up close is challenging. This was the mission of the *Parker Solar Probe*, which launched from Earth in August 2018. Earth is about 93 million miles (150 million km) from the sun. The *Parker Solar Probe* is designed to travel as close to the sun as

3.83 million miles (6.16 million km). To survive the heat, the probe is equipped with a heavy-duty heat shield. It must keep the heat shield facing the sun to avoid overheating.

The probe gathers data about the particles coming from the sun. It also studies the sun's magnetic field. The probe will help scientists learn more about how the sun works. Its data may help improve forecasting of solar flares and other events on the sun that affect life on Earth.

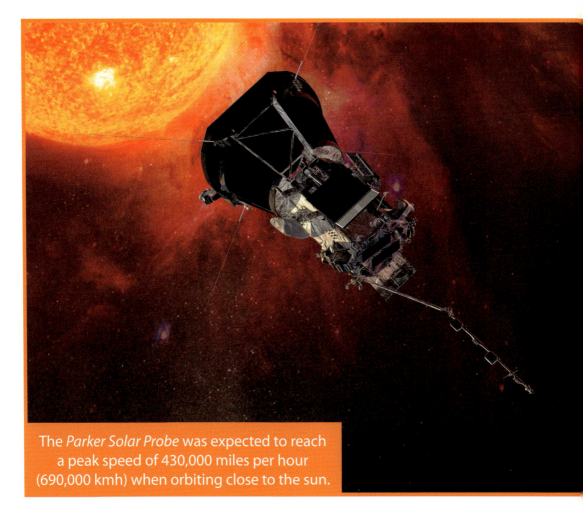

The *Parker Solar Probe* was expected to reach a peak speed of 430,000 miles per hour (690,000 kmh) when orbiting close to the sun.

THE SUN

LIGHT SHOWS

The sun plays a role in a few impressive displays that are visible to people on Earth. One is a solar eclipse. When three objects in space line up just right, they can block the view of each other. Earth, the sun, and the moon sometimes line up in this way. The moon passes directly between the sun and Earth. For a few minutes, it blocks sunlight, casting an eerie darkness on part of the Earth. People in the affected region are in the moon's shadow.

A composite photograph shows the appearance of the sun before, during, and after a solar eclipse.

Special protective glasses are needed to safely observe an eclipse.

   Viewers should be careful when looking at a solar eclipse. Looking at the sun can damage the eyes, even with sunglasses on and during an eclipse. Regular sunglasses do not offer enough protection. People must use eye protection specifically designed for looking at eclipses.

THE SUN

The southern lights as seen from New Zealand

Another fascinating light show is an aurora. The aurora borealis, also called the northern lights, are seen near the north pole. The aurora australis, also called the southern lights, are visible near the south pole. Auroras are swirling natural displays of glowing light in shades of red, green, purple, pink, and yellow. They occur during fall and winter nights.

Auroras appear on other planets, too.

Auroras are caused by particles from the sun, known as the solar wind, striking Earth. When they hit atoms of gas high in the atmosphere, the particles strip electrons away from the gas. The result is a glowing color. Striking oxygen causes red or green light, and striking nitrogen causes green and purple light.

Astronauts in space get incredible views of auroras.

PLANETS

A disk of material around the young sun eventually formed the planets.

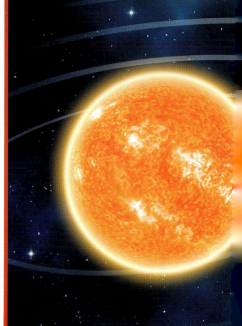

Eight planets orbit the sun. Scientists are not certain how they formed. The most widely accepted idea is that they formed along with the sun about 4.6 billion years ago. When the solar nebula created the sun, there was still material left over. This material orbited the sun in a disk shape. Over millions of years, gravity gathered that material into the planets we know today.

Rocky planets formed in the warm region close to the sun, in the inner solar system. Planets made of gas formed in the colder outer solar system. Particles coming from the sun blew away most of the leftover gas and dust.

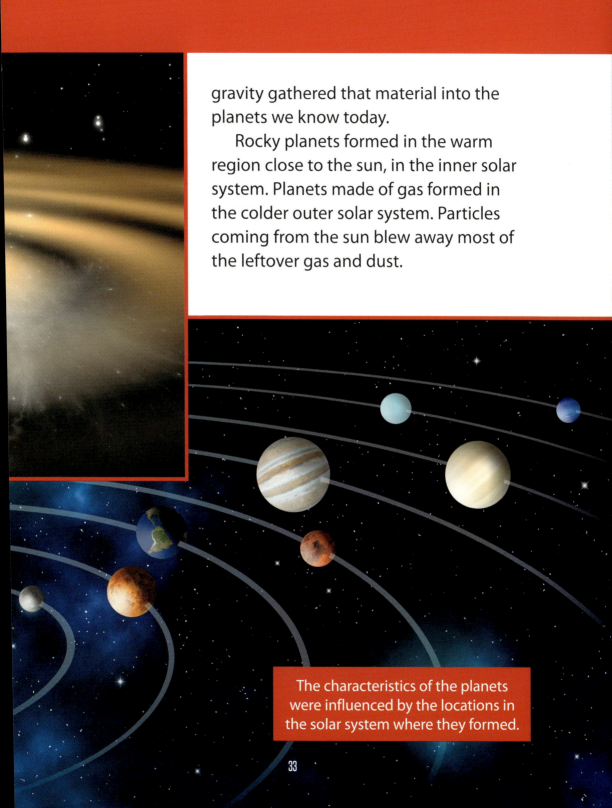

The characteristics of the planets were influenced by the locations in the solar system where they formed.

PLANETS

The outermost planets are the gas giants Jupiter, Saturn, Uranus, and Neptune. Scientists believe they formed first. The cold of this region slowed the movement of gases, which allowed them to be drawn into the growing planets' gravity. Scientists estimate that Jupiter and Saturn formed relatively quickly, in about ten million years. Uranus and Neptune trailed not far behind.

The solar system's gas giants are made up of gases blown by powerful winds.

The terrestrial planets have hard surfaces that spacecraft can land on.

The inner planets have rocky surfaces and are known as the terrestrial planets. They are Mercury, Venus, Earth, and Mars. Not much gas was left after forming the faraway cold planets. The terrestrial planets, located closer to the sun, are warmer and smaller. Scientists believe they may have taken tens of millions of years to form.

PLANETS

MERCURY

Mercury is the solar system's smallest planet. It has a gradually cooling iron core. The planet has shrunk slightly as the core has cooled, buckling the surface into jagged cliffs and forming a valley larger than Earth's Grand Canyon. Scientists estimate it has shrunk by roughly 3 to 6 miles (5 to 10 km) in diameter since it formed.

Mercury is an airless world marked by many craters.

As the closest planet to the sun, Mercury has the shortest orbit. This also makes it the fastest planet, zipping along at about 29 miles (47 km) per second. The planet was named for the Roman wing-shoed messenger god. Mercury completes an orbit around the sun in just 88 days, compared with about 365 days for Earth. However, Mercury rotates on its axis much more slowly. A rotation on Earth takes 24 hours. On Mercury it takes 1,416 hours, or 59 Earth days. This means that on Mercury, a year passes in less than two days. Mercury has no moons.

Mercury's location closest to the sun means that it experiences very intense sunlight.

VENUS

Venus was the first planet visited by a spacecraft from Earth. The US *Mariner 2*

Venus is covered in thick clouds, but spacecraft can use sensors to peer through to the surface beneath.

spacecraft flew past it in 1962. It found that Venus is covered by poisonous clouds that rain sulfuric acid. The surface roasts at a temperature of 900 degrees Fahrenheit (482°C), making Venus the hottest planet in the solar system. The thick atmosphere pushes with so much air pressure that standing on Venus would be like being 1 mile (1.6 km) deep in Earth's oceans.

Most planets rotate counterclockwise. Rusty-colored Venus spins clockwise, which means the sun rises in the west and sets in the east. A collision with another body in the distant past may have reversed its direction. Venus rotates slowly, once every 243 Earth days. The planet takes 225 days to complete an orbit, meaning its day is longer than its year. Although Venus formed billions of years ago, researchers believe some of its surface features were created much more recently, perhaps just 150 million years ago. Scientists aren't sure why. Like Mercury, Venus has no moons.

Venus was named for the Roman goddess of love and beauty. It is alone among the planets in being named for a goddess. Venus is the brightest object in the night sky after the sun and moon.

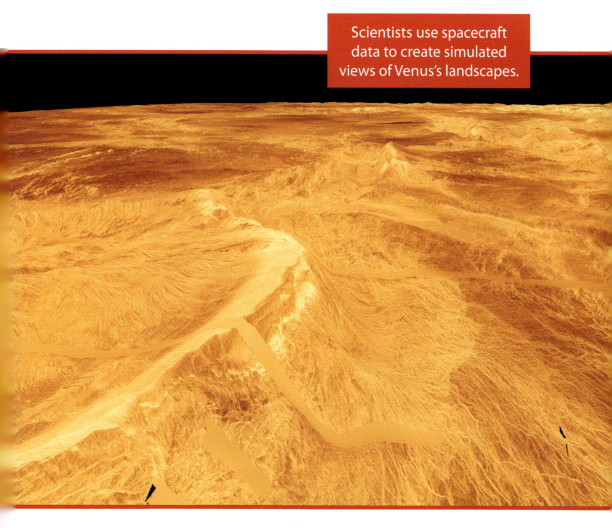

Scientists use spacecraft data to create simulated views of Venus's landscapes.

PLANETS

EARTH

The name *Earth* comes from the German word for *ground*. Earth has many features that make it an ideal place for supporting life as we know it. It is 70 percent water, providing an abundant supply of a substance living things need to survive. The atmosphere contains the oxygen animals require for breathing and the carbon dioxide plants need for carrying

A weather satellite captured this view of one-half of Earth's surface.

After the sun, the moon is the brightest object that appears in Earth's sky.

out photosynthesis. The atmosphere also holds in the sun's warmth, keeping much of the planet at a livable temperature. Earth's magnetic field helps protect the surface from harmful particles from the sun, and the thick atmosphere causes most meteoroids to burn up before they can strike the ground and cause damage.

Earth completes one orbit around the sun in slightly more than 365 days. Each revolution on its axis takes about 24 hours. Earth's axis is tilted about 23.5 degrees, meaning that parts of the globe receive more or less direct sunlight over the course of a year. This is what creates the planet's seasons.

Earth has a single moon. In English it is simply called "the moon." Its Latin name, Luna, is the source of terms like *lunar*. In Greek it is Selene. This is the source of the term *selenology*, the study of the moon's geology.

PLANETS

MARS

Mars was named for the Roman god of war because of its blood-red color. Aside from Earth, Mars is the most explored planet. It is relatively close to Earth, and spacecraft are able to land on its surface. In 1965, the US space agency, the National Aeronautics and Space Administration (NASA), sent *Mariner 4* on a successful flyby mission to Mars. Since then, many more orbiters, landers, and rovers have visited the planet and sent back images and other valuable data. Mars is smaller than Earth, but the two planets share some things in common. Like Earth, Mars experiences seasons and has polar ice caps. Water may have flowed on the planet's surface.

Mars's atmosphere is extremely thin and composed mainly of carbon dioxide. The planet is also very cold.

Small polar ice caps are visible on Mars.

Temperatures average -80 degrees Fahrenheit (-62°C) but can drop to -195 degrees Fahrenheit (-126°C). Winds blowing across its surface stir up dust storms that sometimes cover the entire planet. Mars's two potato-shaped moons, Phobos and Deimos, were discovered in 1877.

A day on Mars is similar to an Earth day. It lasts a bit more than 24 hours. However, the more distant orbit of Mars means that its year is much longer. It takes Mars about 687 Earth days to complete an orbit of the sun.

Phobos, *left*, and Deimos, *right*, are small and have irregular shapes.

PLANETS

Jupiter is by far the solar system's largest planet.

JUPITER

Jupiter, the largest of the planets and one of the brightest in the night sky, was named for the king of the Roman gods. All the other planets combined have only half Jupiter's mass. If Earth were nickel-size, Jupiter would be basketball-size. The gas giant is draped in bands of reddish brown, orange, and yellow. These bands are clouds composed of ammonia and water floating through an atmosphere of hydrogen and helium gases. A centuries-long storm larger than Earth, known as the planet's Great Red Spot, rages through the clouds. Jupiter has no real surface below its swirling gases.

Without a solid surface, life is unlikely to exist on Jupiter. But scientists believe that one of its moons, Europa, could potentially support life. It appears to have seas of liquid water under its icy crust. It is one of more than 70 moons of Jupiter that have been discovered. More are still being found today. Amateur astronomer Kai Ly found a new one in 2021 by studying old pictures of the planet. Jupiter spins quickly, completing a rotation about every ten hours. It takes about 11.9 Earth years for it to complete one orbit around the sun.

Europa is one of Jupiter's many fascinating moons.

PLANETS

Saturn's striking rings make the planet instantly recognizable.

SATURN

Saturn, the second-largest planet in the solar system, is known for its spectacular rings. Although the rings are only a few meters in height, they stretch 175,000 miles (280,000 km) from Saturn. Scientists believe that the planet's gravity broke apart comets, asteroids, or chunks of moons. The pieces splintered into billions of pieces of ice, rock, and dust, orbiting the planet and becoming its rings. Most pieces are small, but a few are as large as mountains.

Like Jupiter, Saturn is a swirl of hydrogen and helium with no real surface. Saturn takes 10.7 hours to complete a rotation

The hazy moon Titan is seen passing in front of Saturn.

on its axis. It takes more than 29 Earth years to orbit the sun. With an axis tilted similarly to Earth's, Saturn has seasons. The planet was named for the Roman god of agriculture and wealth.

Saturn also has many moons. Astronomers have identified 82, with the possibility of more that have not yet been discovered. Moons Enceladus and Titan both have water, and scientists think they have the potential to support life.

PLANETS

URANUS

Uranus, named for the Greek god of the sky, orbits the sun while rotating on its side. The tilt of its axis is almost 90 degrees. Scientists believe a collision with a large object may have knocked Uranus into that tilt long ago. The planet's unusual tilt causes extreme seasons.

A day on Uranus equals just over 17 Earth hours. One year is roughly 84 Earth years. This means that winter lasts 21 years. During this time, the planet's poles receive the most direct

Photos of Uranus show a nearly featureless light-blue world.

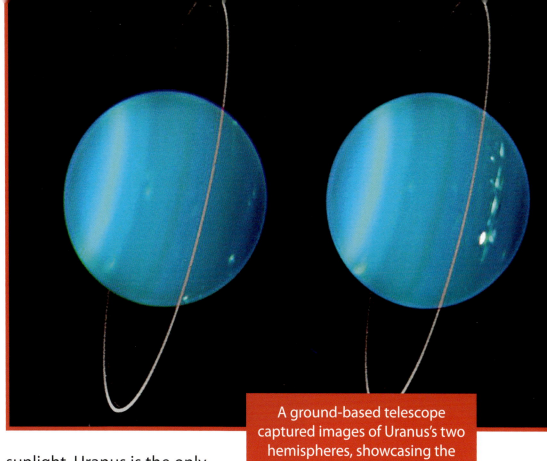

A ground-based telescope captured images of Uranus's two hemispheres, showcasing the planet's rings and its steep tilt.

sunlight. Uranus is the only planet besides Venus that rotates clockwise.

Like other gas giants, Uranus doesn't have a surface. But because the planet is so cold, most of the gas has become a whirling mass of thick liquids and ice. Uranus has strong winds and air pressure, so a spacecraft flying into the planet would quickly be destroyed.

Some of Uranus's 27 moons may have buried oceans. Scientists wonder if this might allow them to support life. Only one spacecraft has made a close approach to Uranus. Future missions might unlock more of the secrets of this frigid planet and its moons.

PLANETS

NEPTUNE

Neptune has stormy weather and freezing temperatures. Winds blowing at more than 1,200 miles per hour (1,900 kmh) make Neptune the windiest planet. Earth's top recorded winds hit only 250 miles per hour (400 kmh).

Like other gas giants, Neptune has a solid core topped with thick layers of gases. As with Uranus, the extremely cold temperatures turn these gases into ice. For this reason, Uranus and Neptune are sometimes called ice giants.

Pictures of Neptune show the deep blue of its atmosphere. Because of this coloring, it was named for the Roman god of the sea. Neptune spins on its axis in 16 hours, and it takes about 165 Earth years to orbit the sun. In 2011, it completed one full year since its discovery in 1846.

Only one spacecraft, *Voyager 2*, has made a close approach to Neptune.

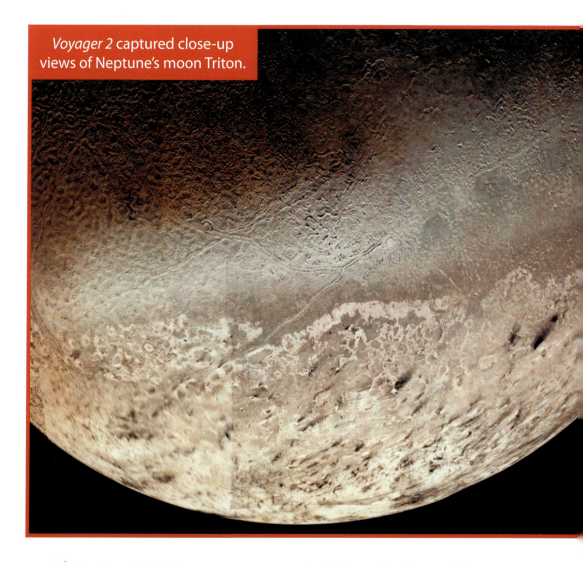

Voyager 2 captured close-up views of Neptune's moon Triton.

Of Neptune's 14 known moons, only Triton, the largest, is spherical. The others are not completely round. Triton orbits Neptune in the opposite direction from Neptune's orbit, making it the only large moon in the solar system known to do so. This suggests it might have once been an independent object and was captured by Neptune's gravity.

PLANETS

DWARF PLANETS

Eight planets make up the solar system. Once there were nine, with tiny Pluto far beyond the orbit of Neptune. But this changed in 2006. The definition of a planet was simple before that year. If it orbited the sun, was a sphere, and was bigger than any orbiting moons, it was a planet. However, astronomers began discovering more objects that met this description in the distant region of the solar system known as the Kuiper belt. It seemed as though the number of planets would soon increase.

Pluto, long classified as a planet, became one of the first dwarf planets in 2006.

In 2006, the International Astronomical Union (IAU) announced a new definition of a planet, as well as a new category: dwarf planets. Besides the earlier elements of the definition, a planet also needed to have gravity strong enough to clear its orbit of other objects. Pluto did not fit this rule, so it became classified as a dwarf planet.

The IAU's decision didn't end the debate. Some scientists want simpler definitions, while others urge for more complicated ones. A simpler definition of planets might bring the five dwarf planets to the planet list. It could also push the number of planets past 100. Scientists will likely keep adjusting their definitions as they learn more.

Scientists continue to search the Kuiper belt for dwarf planets and other objects.

PLANETS

    Pluto was discovered in 1930. Like other dwarf planets, Pluto is smaller than Earth's moon. About 1,400 miles (2,250 km) wide, Pluto would cover about half of the United States. Pluto takes about 6.4 Earth days to complete one rotation on its axis. With 3.7 billion miles (5.9 billion km) between it and the sun, a year lasts 248 Earth years. An average temperature of -387 degrees Fahrenheit (-233°C) makes it unlikely to support life.

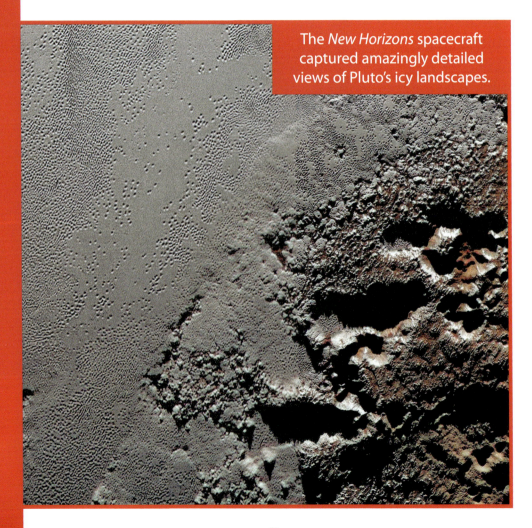

The *New Horizons* spacecraft captured amazingly detailed views of Pluto's icy landscapes.

With the powerful telescopes of the 1990s, astronomers saw more faint, distant objects orbiting the sun. Many of these icy objects were clustered in the Kuiper belt. Eris, Haumea, and Makemake are other dwarf planets in the Kuiper belt. Little is known about them yet because of their great distance from Earth. Another dwarf planet, Ceres, is located in the asteroid belt, a region located between the orbits of Mars and Jupiter. Continuing discoveries may eventually expand the dwarf planet list to include thousands of objects.

Ceres was once considered an asteroid but later was classified as a dwarf planet.

PLANETS

An artist's impression shows Earth next to the exoplanet Kepler-1649c.

EXOPLANETS

Many stars have planets orbiting them. These planets in other solar systems are known as exoplanets. It's hard to see exoplanets because of the glare from the stars they orbit. Still, NASA has counted thousands. Scientists have developed multiple methods of finding them. For example, if a star grows dim, this may indicate that an exoplanet is briefly blocking it from view. If the dimming occurs on a regular basis, it likely indicates an orbiting exoplanet. Astronomers may also detect the influence of an exoplanet's gravity on its star.

   Scientists believe they will discover many thousands of additional exoplanets. Exoplanets vary in size and conditions, just as the planets in our solar system do. Some orbit in systems with two or even three stars. Some, known as rogue planets, orbit no star at all. They drift through deep space alone.

Aside from the sun, the nearest star with at least one exoplanet orbiting it is Proxima Centauri. It is about 25 trillion miles (40 trillion km) from Earth. With this great distance, it is unlikely that people will be able do any first-hand exploration of it or any other exoplanets anytime soon.

Space telescopes play an important role in discovering new exoplanets.

THE MOON

The people of ancient Greece and some earlier civilizations thought the moon was one of many gods. Others thought it was a resting place for the dead who would later be reborn. However, one ancient Greek philosopher who lived 2,500 years ago took a more scientific approach to the moon. Anaxagoras believed that carefully watching an object would lead him to its truth. Particularly interested in astronomy, Anaxagoras said that the moon was not a god. It was a rock like Earth. Mountains rise from its surface. It gets its light from the sun. He used what he learned to explain other lunar phenomena, such as eclipses and moon phases. But these ideas were not pleasing to other powerful

The moon's prominent place in the night sky inspired ancient thinkers to consider its true nature.

Greeks, who felt it was an attack on their religion. Anaxagoras was sentenced to death, a punishment that later changed to exile. His ideas, though, would inform future scientists.

Anaxagoras would later have a crater on the moon named after him.

THE MOON

WHAT THE MOON IS MADE OF

Saying that the moon is made of cheese used to be a popular joke. One early source of this idea comes from the 1546 book *The Proverbs of John Heywood*. The book lists Heywood's sayings, including some that remain common today, such as "the more, the merrier" and "a penny for your thoughts." One passage in the book says that "the moon is made of greene cheese."

Before spacecraft and astronauts visited the moon, astronomers could only make guesses about its exact composition.

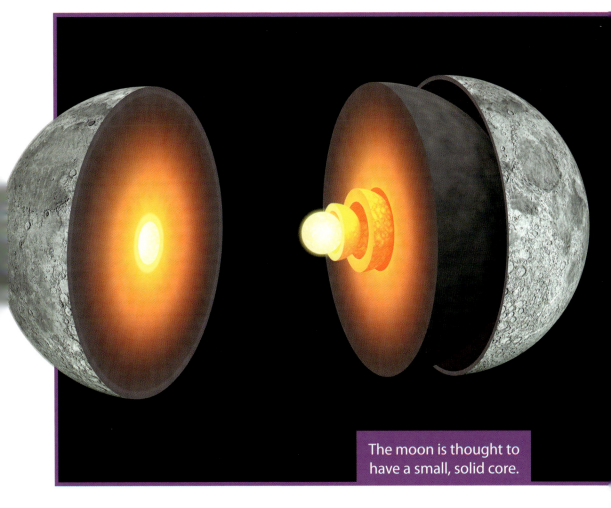

The moon is thought to have a small, solid core.

Scientists know that the moon's surface is loose rock and dust covering inactive volcanoes, hardened lava flows, and craters where it was hit by other objects in space. With no wind or water to weather it, the dust has razor-sharp edges. As with Earth, the moon's surface covers a mantle, a thick solid layer beneath the surface. The moon's mantle is made of minerals. Below that, the hot, melted layers of the outer core wrap around a small metallic inner core of iron and nickel.

THE MOON

The moon is a desolate, airless place.

The moon doesn't have an atmosphere. Instead, it has an exosphere, which is an extremely thin layer of gases surrounding the moon. The molecules are so thinly spread that they seldom bump each other.

While the moon doesn't have seasons, it moves through extremes from 260 degrees Fahrenheit (127°C) in sunlight to -280 degrees Fahrenheit (-173°C) in shadow. Daytime lasts 13.5 days and nighttime the same. Some parts of the surface, shadowed by craters, never get sunlight. Using radar, scientists have found water in one of these regions at the moon's north pole.

A composite image shows the moon's northern hemisphere, with the north pole at the center.

BIRTH OF THE MOON

Studying rocks gathered from missions to the moon helped give people clues to the moon's origin. The missions have collected hundreds of pounds of rock and soil samples. The samples show that Earth and the moon have much of their makeup in common. This tells scientists that, despite the two bodies' differences, their histories are likely linked.

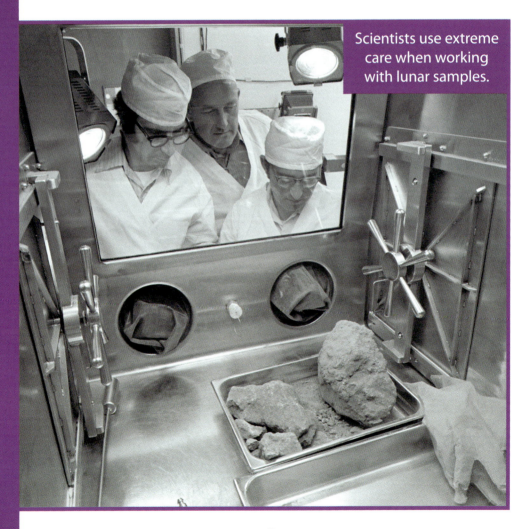

Scientists use extreme care when working with lunar samples.

The most widely accepted theory regarding the moon's origin is that a giant impact created it. Scientists believe that early in Earth's development, another small planet crashed into it. This planet, called Theia, is thought to have been about the size of Mars. The crash caused both planets to melt. Gravity pulled much of Theia's mass into Earth, but a large piece was knocked into orbit and became Earth's moon. The moon is slightly more than one-fourth the diameter of Earth.

The collision between Earth and Theia would have been an incredibly violent event.

The moon orbits Earth once every 27 days. It takes only slightly longer to rotate on its axis, about 27.3 days. Over time, Earth's powerful gravity has caused the same side of the moon to always face Earth. This phenomenon is known as tidal locking.

THE MOON

Even when the moon is mostly dark, a close look can reveal features on the unlit portion.

MOON PHASES

The moon seems to shine at night, but this light does not come from the moon itself. Instead, this is reflected light from the sun. Sunlight always lights half of the moon, but from Earth, the lit portion of the moon is determined by where it is in its orbit. Sometimes the moon appears as a full circle. Other times it looks like a thin crescent. Sometimes the moon is not visible at all. These different views are called moon phases.

The phase when the moon can't be seen is called a new moon. At this time, the sun is shining only on the side of the moon facing away from Earth. In the waxing crescent phase, only a sliver of the moon is visible. People on Earth can see only a bit of the moon's daylight side. Each day, the slice of the moon that people can see waxes, or grows larger. Eventually, half of the moon is lit up. This phase is called its first quarter. A moon in the gibbous waxing phase appears to be swelling, with the light spreading to cover more than half its visible face.

As more of the moon becomes visible, Earth receives more of its reflected light.

THE MOON

At the time of the full moon, the moon's entire sunlit side is visible on Earth as a full circle. People call the full moon by lots of different names, depending on the season. These names include harvest moon, beaver moon, and flower moon. After the full moon, the process runs in reverse. The sunlit portion of the moon shrinks during the waning gibbous phase. At the last quarter, half the moon is lit. In the waning crescent phase, the visible slice of the moon gets thinner and thinner. Eventually the entire moon is dark. The sequence begins again with the new moon phase.

The moon is harder to see in the daytime, but it is often still possible to spot it.

MOON

The moon is often visible during the day, especially during the first or last quarter, though it is always dimmer than at night. In the new moon phase, however, it is invisible in the daytime sky. And in the full moon phase, it is below the horizon during the daytime, so it can't be seen.

The moon is usually white with some shadowy gray. But it can also appear in many colors. During a lunar eclipse, the moon passes into Earth's shadow. Not all the light is blocked, though. Some light passing through Earth's atmosphere strikes the moon, giving it a red color. Smoke from wildfires can also make the moon look red. The moon may look yellow or orange when near the horizon. At times, the moon even has a pinkish or purple glow. From beyond Earth's atmosphere, the moon looks brownish gray.

The effects of Earth's atmosphere sometimes give the moon unusual colors.

THE MOON

THE MOON'S EFFECTS ON EARTH

The moon does more than provide a source of light during cloudless nights on Earth. It also affects Earth's motion, its seas, and its plant and animal life. It has played key roles in the history of human civilization, too.

The phases of the moon can be seen on a Roman mosaic from the 200s CE.

The moon helps keep Earth stable in its orbit.

The moon is relatively large compared with Earth. As a result, its gravity helps hold Earth steady. Other terrestrial planets without large moons wobble in their orbits, with the poles shifting around over time. This can cause unpredictable changes in climate. Thanks to the moon, this does not happen to Earth. The moon's gravity keeps Earth's climate stable.

THE MOON

The tides are among the most visible effects that the moon has on Earth.

The moon's control of ocean tides is a well-known example of the moon's effect on Earth. The moon's gravity tugs on land and sea, but the tug on land is hard to notice without specialized instruments. The ocean is another matter. The moon's gravity pulls at the ocean on the side of Earth facing the moon, creating high tides. This happens most during new or full moons. That's because the moon, Earth, and sun are all lined up at those times, so the water is affected by the combined gravity

of the moon and the sun. Tides on part of the globe are low when that part is turned away from the moon. Most parts of the world have two high tides and two low tides each day.

The shifting tides have a significant impact on animal life along the world's coastlines.

THE MOON

    Studies show that birds are more active hunters during a bright moon and migrate following a full moon. Birds also show increased singing and communication with each other during a full moon. Tiny crustaceans called sand hoppers track moon changes with their antennae. They hide beneath beach sands by day. At night, during low tide, they search for food. Even corals in the oceans release their eggs following a fall full moon.

A full moon can influence bird behaviors, including migration.

The joint pine is native to Europe and Africa.

The joint pine plant is another example of the moon's effect on life. It needs insects to carry its pollen so that it can reproduce. Unlike other kinds of plants, however, it has no flowers to attract insects. Instead, under a bright moon, it creates tiny, sticky drops of fluid that shine in the moonlight. Insects are drawn to it and soon carry the pollen away within the fluid. This plant depends on the moon for reproduction.

THE MOON

The moon was also the basis for timekeeping in some of the earliest civilizations. The earliest lunar calendar was discovered in cave art in France and Germany. The calendars date back to 32,000 BCE, a time known as the late Upper Paleolithic period.

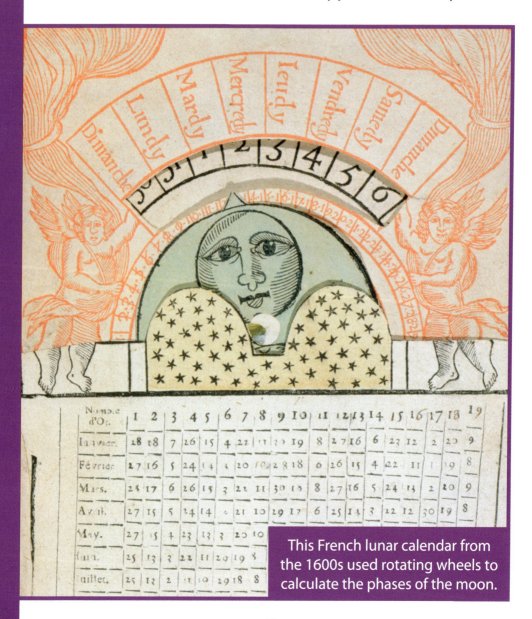

This French lunar calendar from the 1600s used rotating wheels to calculate the phases of the moon.

Parades for lunar new year celebrations are held in Chinese communities around the world.

The calendars were also carved into small stones and animal bones or antlers. These were like extremely early versions of today's pocket calendars. These marks and carvings show the different phases of the moon. Keeping track of the days and seasons would have been particularly helpful for long hunting trips.

Many lunar calendars today make some adjustments based on the sun, and they are more properly called lunisolar calendars. Most of the world, including the United States, has adopted the solar Gregorian calendar. This calendar developed from the Roman lunar calendar. But many people still use lunar or lunisolar calendars to establish the dates of holidays. These include the Hebrew, Hindu, and Islamic religions, as well as several cultures in East Asia.

SPACE EXPLORATION

During World War II (1939–1945), German engineers led by Wernher von Braun developed the V-2 rocket. It was the most advanced rocket design the world had yet seen. Von Braun's dream was to build rockets to explore space. But before

Wernher von Braun, one of history's most important rocket engineers, got his start working for Nazi Germany.

V-2 rockets devastated the spots where they landed.

and during the war, the Nazi Party controlled Germany. Von Braun and his team developed rockets to use as weapons of war. Slave labor was used to build these weapons, and the rockets carried bombs into civilian targets. Thousands of people were killed.

As the war drew to a close, the Soviet Union invaded Germany from the east and the United States and United Kingdom entered from the west. German rocket scientists began surrendering to these armies. Some scientists went to the Soviet Union. Others, including von Braun, went to the United States. These scientists helped the Soviet Union and the United States develop advanced rockets in the postwar era. This time, many of the rockets would be used to explore space.

Von Braun, *wearing cast*, surrendered to the United States when Germany lost the war.

In addition to gathering German scientists, the United States also seized rockets and parts from Germany's abandoned factories and launch sites. The United States began testing V-2 rockets in 1946. For a 1949 test, a small US rocket was placed atop a V-2 rocket. This second stage fired after the V-2 rocket expended its own fuel, pushing the small rocket even higher. This test reached an altitude of 244 miles (393 km), becoming the first human-made object to enter space. However, it did not enter orbit around Earth. It flew up and then fell back to Earth.

US scientists tested captured V-2 rocket technology in the late 1940s.

SPACE EXPLORATION

THE SPACE RACE

The United States and the Soviet Union fought on the same side during World War II, but tensions between the two nations grew after the war. They entered a period known as the Cold War. During this conflict, they competed for power and influence rather than fighting each other directly. Part of this competition involved working toward notable accomplishments in space exploration. Achieving these first would enhance national prestige. The competition became known as the Space Race.

Many people in the United States believed their nation possessed more advanced technology than the Soviet Union. They were shocked when the Soviets launched the first satellite, *Sputnik*, into Earth orbit in October 1957.

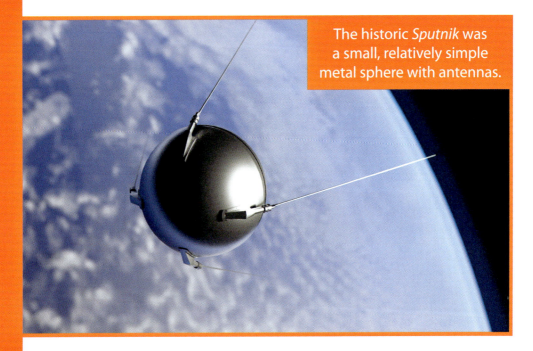

The historic *Sputnik* was a small, relatively simple metal sphere with antennas.

The launch of *Explorer I* gave the United States its first success in space.

Many worried that if the Soviet Union could launch a satellite into orbit, it could also launch weapons to the United States.

The United States was determined to catch up. In December, the United States attempted to launch its own satellite. The rocket lifted off and then stopped two seconds after launch, exploding in a massive fireball. In January 1958, the United States succeeded with its *Explorer I* satellite. The spacecraft went on to discover the Van Allen Belts, a band of radiation around Earth.

SPACE EXPLORATION

The Soviets achieved another first by sending a probe to the moon in 1959. A probe is a spacecraft carrying instruments to send information back to Earth but no humans. Then, the Soviet Union achieved the biggest space achievement yet by launching a person into space. Cosmonaut Yuri Gagarin orbited Earth on April 12, 1961. He safely reentered the atmosphere and parachuted to the ground. Just a few weeks later, the United States launched its first astronaut, Alan Shepard, into space aboard the spacecraft *Freedom 7*. However, the Redstone rocket that launched Shepard did not have enough power to reach orbit. His flight was a suborbital mission, flying in a high arc and returning to Earth.

Alan Shepard prepares for liftoff in the cramped *Freedom 7* capsule.

US space missions in the 1960s often ended in a splashdown in the ocean.

Over the next several years, each nation launched more ambitious missions that built on their successes. They launched new spacecraft that could accommodate multiple astronauts. They developed ways to have two spacecraft meet up in orbit. The world's first space walk, carried out by Soviet cosmonaut Alexei Leonov, was in March 1965. The United States and the Soviet Union were both working toward the same long-term goal—landing a person on the moon.

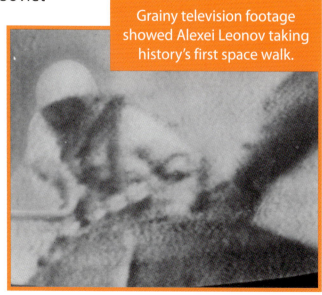

Grainy television footage showed Alexei Leonov taking history's first space walk.

SPACE EXPLORATION

The enormous Saturn V rocket carried the Apollo astronauts to the moon.

Major failures during tests of its large rockets set back the Soviet moon program. The United States achieved the first moon landing during the Apollo 11 mission in 1969. Astronaut Neil Armstrong became the first person to walk on the moon. Five more US moon landings followed. The rock and soil samples astronauts brought back, along with the scientific instruments they placed on the lunar surface, helped teach scientists a great deal about the moon's history and structure.

Tensions between the Soviet Union and the United States began to ease during the 1970s. The two nations agreed to carry out a joint mission in 1975. A US Apollo spacecraft and a Soviet Soyuz spacecraft met up in orbit. During the mission, the astronauts and cosmonauts exchanged gifts and performed joint science experiments. A photo of astronaut Tom Stafford shaking hands with cosmonaut Alexei Leonov symbolized a new era of international cooperation in space.

Later Apollo missions included an electric car called the lunar roving vehicle.

The crews of the Apollo-Soyuz mission posed for a photo with a model of their spacecraft before the flight.

SPACE EXPLORATION

EXPLORING THE SOLAR SYSTEM

In addition to their crewed space programs, both major space powers worked to explore the solar system with robotic probes. The Soviet Union sent a series of missions to Venus as part of the Venera program. While the early attempts failed, *Venera 4* entered Venus's atmosphere and sent back data to Earth in 1967.

Venera 8 descended to the surface of Venus using a parachute.

Some probes in the program were designed to orbit Venus, while others were meant to land. A few successful landers sent back data from the planet's surface before being destroyed by the atmosphere's scorching temperatures and crushing pressure. Their data included photos, temperature and wind readings, and other information that suggested Venus would not support life.

The brutal conditions on Venus meant that probes could not survive long before they ceased functioning.

SPACE EXPLORATION

The Soviets also launched rovers, landing them on the moon in 1970 and 1973. The solar-powered vehicles traveled the moon's surface, taking pictures and collecting data. Controllers directed them from Earth. In 1996, NASA sent *Sojourner*, the first of several rovers to explore Mars. It was followed in 2004 by the twin rovers *Spirit* and *Opportunity*. These rovers were about the size of golf carts.

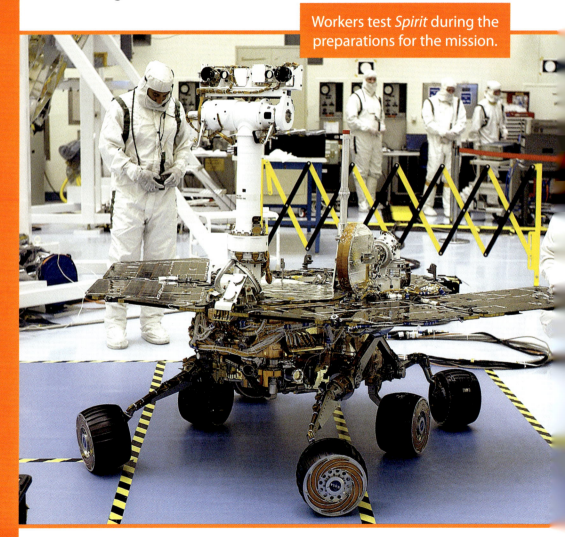

Workers test *Spirit* during the preparations for the mission.

Perseverance and *Ingenuity* brought the most sophisticated scientific instruments yet to the surface of Mars.

In 2012, the car-size *Curiosity* landed on Mars. Another lander sharing the same basic design, *Perseverance*, landed in February 2021. It carried with it a small helicopter, *Ingenuity*, to test out flying a vehicle in Mars's thin atmosphere. The tests were successful, showing how flying vehicles may be useful in the future exploration of Mars.

SPACE EXPLORATION

The United States launched deep-space probes in the 1970s. The most ambitious were *Voyager 1* and *Voyager 2*. These identical spacecraft were launched a few weeks apart in 1977. The missions took advantage of a rare alignment of the planets of the outer solar system. *Voyager 1* flew past Jupiter and Saturn. *Voyager 2* also visited Jupiter and Saturn, but its path allowed it to continue to Uranus and Neptune.

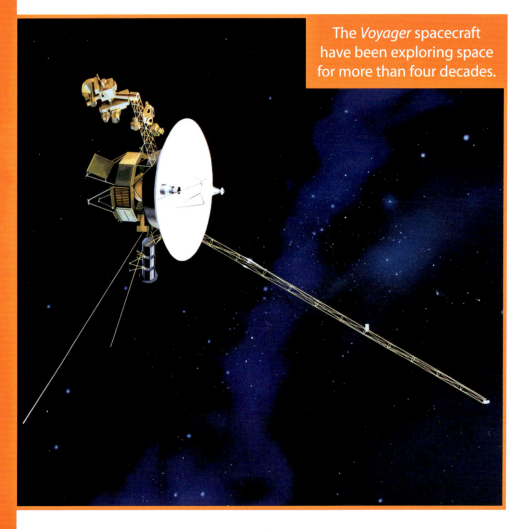

The *Voyager* spacecraft have been exploring space for more than four decades.

Voyager 1 sent back close-up photos of Jupiter's four largest moons, *clockwise from top right*, Europa, Callisto, Ganymede, and Io.

The missions sent back valuable images and other data about the worlds of the outer solar system. After exploring the planets, the *Voyager* spacecraft continued outward into space. They have sent back data from the edge of the solar system. Scientists expect that the power sources of the probes will last well into the 2030s. Even once they can no longer send signals, the *Voyager* probes will continue to silently travel through space.

SPACE EXPLORATION

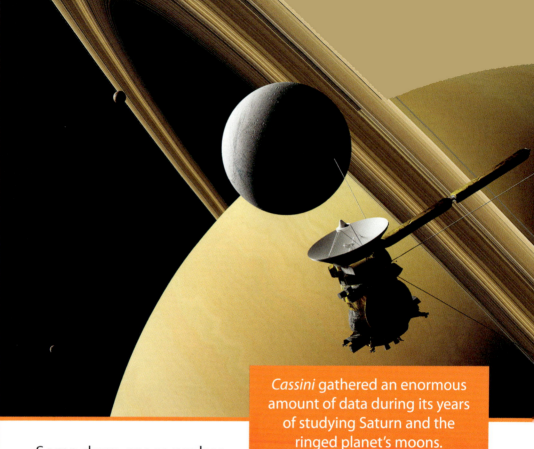

Cassini gathered an enormous amount of data during its years of studying Saturn and the ringed planet's moons.

Some deep-space probes were international efforts. One such spacecraft was *Cassini*, launched in 1997. A project of NASA, the European Space Agency (ESA), and the Italian Space Agency, the *Cassini* probe was designed to study Saturn and its moons. It reached the ringed planet in 2004. It entered Saturn's orbit and remained there for more than a decade. *Cassini* captured stunning photos of Saturn. It also collected a wealth of scientific information, including evidence that the moon Enceladus could potentially support life in its oceans.

Cassini carried with it the ESA's *Huygens* probe. *Huygens* was dropped into the atmosphere of Titan, becoming the first spacecraft to make a landing in the outer solar system.

It relayed information about Titan's surface, sending back photos from the ground.

In 2017, *Cassini* was running low on fuel. Mission controllers commanded the probe to plunge into Saturn's atmosphere, intentionally destroying it. This would prevent the possibility of the probe losing control and crashing into one of Saturn's moons. If there was any chance of Enceladus having life, they didn't want to risk the chance of contaminating it with anything *Cassini* brought from Earth.

Huygens made the most distant landing in the history of space exploration to date.

SPACE STATIONS

During the Space Race era, the Soviets focused on creating space stations. They launched the unmanned Salyut 1 into orbit in 1971. It was the first space station. Cosmonauts launched to the station later that year. They lived aboard Salyut 1 for three weeks. When they returned to Earth, a valve became stuck open during reentry, depressurizing the spacecraft and killing the cosmonauts. But their pioneering mission laid the groundwork for future space stations.

The United States launched its own space station, Skylab, in 1973. Three crews of astronauts lived aboard the station during the next year. They carried out a variety of experiments in fields including biology and astronomy. No additional crews visited the station. The development of the new US spacecraft, the space shuttle, took longer

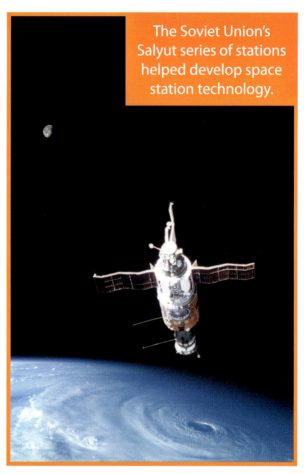

The Soviet Union's Salyut series of stations helped develop space station technology.

The large Skylab station gave astronauts more room to live and work in space than ever before.

than expected. It was not ready in time to visit Skylab and boost the station's orbit. In 1979, the abandoned space station reentered Earth's atmosphere and mostly burned up.

The Soviet Union continued its own space station projects. In 1986, it began constructing a new space station called Mir. After launching the first module, the Soviets added several more over the next few years, creating a larger and more complex space station. In 1991, the Soviet Union collapsed, forming several new nations. The largest, Russia, continued the space program, including the operation of Mir.

Mir was the largest and most complex space station yet.

The station remained in use for more than a decade. US astronauts visited the station a few times, another example of international cooperation in space following the Apollo-Soyuz mission. Russian space authorities put Mir through a controlled deorbit in 2001. Like Skylab, it was intentionally burned up while reentering Earth's atmosphere.

The reentry and breakup of Mir could be seen from the Pacific island nation of Fiji.

NASA astronaut Shannon Lucid, *left*, poses for a photo with cosmonauts Yuriy V. Usachov, *middle*, and Yuriy I. Onufriyenko, *right*, aboard Mir in 1996.

SPACE EXPLORATION

In the 1990s, plans were in progress to create the International Space Station (ISS). The project is headed by the United States and Russia, but it also includes more than a dozen other countries. The first

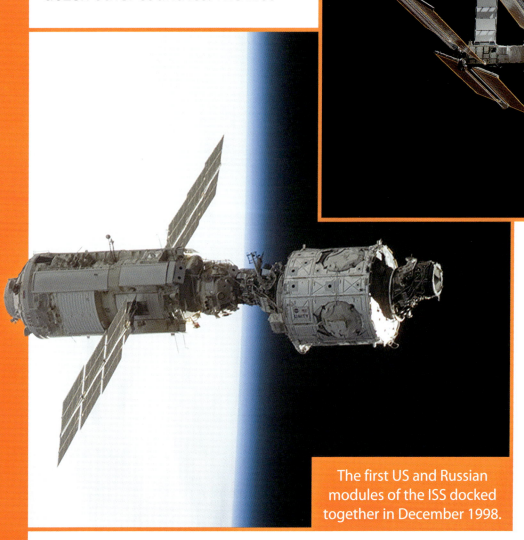

The first US and Russian modules of the ISS docked together in December 1998.

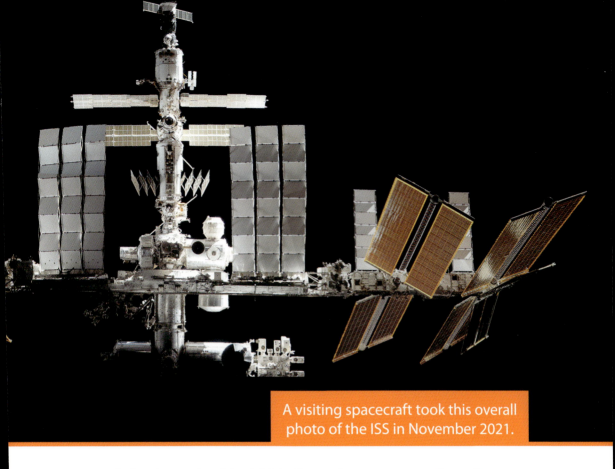

A visiting spacecraft took this overall photo of the ISS in November 2021.

two modules launched in 1998. Over the next two decades, astronauts added more modules, structural elements, and solar panels to generate electricity.

Today the ISS is the size of a football field and can house seven astronauts. Its first crew arrived in 2000, and it has been continuously occupied since then. Crews perform experiments in orbit and learn how to live in space for long periods of time. This work will contribute to future long-duration space missions. The ISS orbits Earth at an altitude of about 250 miles (402 km), speeding along at 17,500 miles per hour (28,000 kmh). The station is expected to be in use until at least 2030.

SPACE EXPLORATION

SHUTTLING INTO SPACE

After the moon landing, NASA looked ahead to the future of space travel. The Apollo missions had been incredibly expensive. One way to bring costs down, making space flight easier and more frequent, would be to use a reusable spacecraft. The result was the space shuttle. This large, airplane-shaped spacecraft had three main rocket engines. It would carry a large fuel tank on its belly. Two huge solid rocket boosters would be strapped to its sides. On the way to orbit, it would drop the boosters and external tank. Then it would return to Earth by gliding like an airplane.

NASA compared the space shuttle to a moving van. It could haul satellites into orbit and transport large

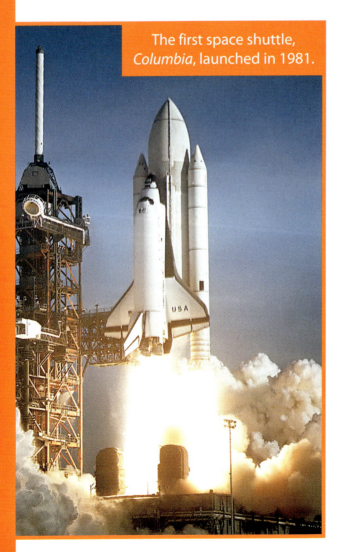

The first space shuttle, *Columbia*, launched in 1981.

Space shuttles landed like airplanes at the end of each mission.

equipment to help build space stations. It could carry up to seven astronauts into space.

In some ways, the shuttle worked as planned. Over 30 years of service, the space shuttles in NASA's fleet made 135 trips to space. In addition to building space stations, their crews repaired satellites and telescopes. Shuttles launched satellites and research laboratories. Astronauts tested new tools and technologies in space.

SPACE EXPLORATION

Astronauts from the space shuttle *Endeavour* repair the Hubble Space Telescope in 1993.

In 1984, astronaut Bruce McCandless became the first astronaut to float freely in space without a tether. He left the space shuttle *Challenger* wearing a backpack called the Manned Maneuvering Unit (MMU). The MMU contained small rocket engines that he could use to fly independently of the shuttle. The test was a success, and he returned safely to *Challenger*. In 1990, the shuttle *Discovery* took the Hubble Space Telescope into space. This telescope would collect stunning pictures of the universe.

Bruce McCandless floats freely using the Manned Maneuvering Unit.

SPACE EXPLORATION

Extensive work needed to be done to the shuttles between missions.

In other ways, the shuttles didn't live up to expectations. Costing $450 million per launch or more, the shuttles weren't the bargain NASA had hoped for. While the shuttles themselves were reusable, parts such as the external fuel tank and the solid rocket boosters had to be replaced or rebuilt each time. NASA aimed to return a shuttle to space within two weeks. But 54 days was their best time. Turnaround times became even longer in the later life of the program.

But the biggest problem with the shuttles was their safety record. In 1986, the shuttle *Challenger* exploded just slightly more than a minute after liftoff. In it were seven astronauts, including Christa McAuliffe, the first civilian space traveler.

McAuliffe was a teacher who hoped to inspire students with her trip. In 2003, the shuttle *Columbia* broke apart as it returned to Earth's atmosphere, killing all seven people on board.

The explosion of the space shuttle *Challenger* demonstrated the risky nature of spaceflight.

SPACE TOURISM

In 2001, American businessman Dennis Tito paid Russia $20 million to ride a Soyuz rocket into space and visit the ISS. This made him history's first space tourist. For Russia, the deal provided needed funds for its space program. Tito described arriving in space as "the greatest moment of [his] life."

Since then, several more space tourism efforts have appeared. The company Virgin Galactic, founded by British billionaire Richard Branson, seeks to give customers a

Space tourist Dennis Tito, *center*, speaks to the press at the Russian mission control center from the ISS.

Blue Origin launched six space tourists in its New Shepard rocket in December 2021.

suborbital ride into space. Blue Origin, the space company created by Amazon founder Jeff Bezos, has also gotten into the suborbital tourism business. Both companies launched their first test flights with people aboard in 2021.

SPACE EXPLORATION

SpaceX has become widely known for its Falcon 9 rocket.

SpaceX, founded by Elon Musk, is also interested in space tourism. In the long term, Musk hopes to make it possible for people to travel to Mars. But in the more immediate future, his company is making strides in Earth orbit. In late 2021, SpaceX sent the first all-civilian crew into orbit. Billionaire Jared Isaacman funded this mission, called Inspiration4, and was its commander. The mission was linked to fundraising efforts for

St. Jude Children's Hospital in Tennessee. By October 2021, the price of a ticket to space ranged from about $450,000 for suborbital flights to approximately $55 million for an orbital mission.

The Inspiration4 mission featured the first all-civilian crew for a space flight.

ASTEROIDS, COMETS, AND METEOROIDS

The ancient Greek philosopher Aristotle was convinced that space was empty beyond the moon. In the 1700s, English scientist and mathematician Isaac Newton agreed that besides the planets and stars, there were no small objects in space. Most thinkers went along with this widely accepted belief. Then, in 1803, more than 3,000 mysterious rocks appeared in the town of L'Aigle in Normandy, France.

Scientist Jean-Baptiste Biot found that the new rocks were unlike existing rocks in the area. Neither factories nor mines

Hundreds of years ago, people did not know what caused meteor showers.

Rocks from space, or meteorites, have a distinctive appearance.

had anything like them, either. However, the rocks were similar to some that had been found in the 1790s. People living in the area all told Biot the same story—the rocks had fallen from the sky. It was clear that the mysterious rocks had come from space. Outer space was not empty after all.

ASTEROIDS, COMETS, AND METEOROIDS

THE SOLAR SYSTEM'S LEFTOVERS

Asteroids, comets, and meteoroids are loose leftovers from the great masses of material that created the planets 4.6 billion years ago. Asteroids are pieces of rock, perhaps with clay or metal mixed in. Scientists believe millions of them, large and small, orbit the sun. Most are located in the asteroid belt between Mars and Jupiter. Occasionally a nearby planet's gravity may throw them into a new orbit. This sends them on a possible collision course with another planet or moon.

Comets are similar to asteroids, but they are typically icier and more distant from the sun. They are made up of dust, ice, and other small bits of material. They travel in an oval-shaped orbit around the sun. Sometimes they cross over planets' orbits

The asteroid belt is home to many millions of asteroids. Some are the size of pebbles, and others are miles across.

on their voyages through the solar system. The longer side of these oval orbits may take them past Pluto. Comets with broad orbits may take 30 million years to finish each trip around the sun. Those that are closer to the sun may complete orbits once in a human lifetime. When a comet approaches the sun, the star's warmth melts some of the comet. Comets contain dust, too. This material flows out behind the comet, forming its tail. Scientists suggest that comet collisions may have delivered water and other materials to Earth in the distant past.

The spacecraft *Rosetta* took up-close photos of a comet.

From Earth, comets' tails form streaks in the night sky.

ASTEROIDS, COMETS, AND METEOROIDS

Meteoroids are chunks of material smaller than asteroids and comets. When asteroids crash into each other, their broken chunks may become meteoroids. So can dust that comes off a comet. When a meteoroid's orbit intersects with Earth, it hits the thick air of the atmosphere and burns up. This creates a brief flash of light known as a meteor, or shooting star. Some meteoroids are large enough that they do not completely burn up. If a piece makes it to the ground, it is known as a meteorite. Most chunks of space rock are no bigger than a person's fist.

Large pieces of intact meteorites are often found in museums.

Few of the rocks that create meteor showers reach the ground.

On nearly any clear night, a person can see a few meteors each hour. When they come at a faster rate than that, it's called a meteor shower. Scientists can usually predict when these showers will occur. They happen when Earth moves through a debris field left behind by a comet or asteroid. Very few meteors survive the trip through Earth's atmosphere to become meteorites. They are too small and delicate. The meteorites found in France from the 1803 shower were rare.

ASTEROIDS, COMETS, AND METEOROIDS

Scientists have identified some meteorites on Earth that originally came from Mars.

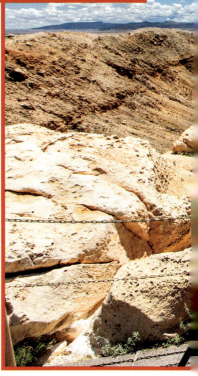

WHEN METEORITES LAND

At first glance, most meteorites look like ordinary Earth rocks. A closer look shows that their surfaces are scarred and pitted from traveling through Earth's atmosphere. Scientists who study them can learn where they came from, what types they are, and their age. Of at least 50,000 meteorites discovered on Earth, 99.8 percent were once asteroids. The remaining 0.2 percent are from Mars and the moon. These were blasted away from Mars and the moon by impacts, flew into space, and eventually fell to Earth.

About 70 percent of Earth is covered by oceans. This means that most meteoroids that make it through Earth's atmosphere fall into water. Rarely, some that do hit land are very large. The Barringer Meteor Crater in Arizona demonstrates the power of these rocks from space. This crater in the Arizona desert is about three-fourths of a mile (1.2 km) wide and 600 feet (180 m) deep. A meteorite strike carved it out of the rock. The impact happened 50,000 years ago, when the land was home to mammoths, mastodons, and giant ground sloths, but not people.

Arizona's Barringer Meteor Crater is a major tourist attraction for the state.

Scientists believe that further back, approximately 65 million years ago, a huge asteroid played a part in the extinction of the dinosaurs. It created a crater 90 miles (145 km) wide in Mexico's Yucatan Peninsula. Such an impact would immediately kill vast numbers of creatures. It would also have a worldwide impact, kicking up enormous clouds of dust that would block the sun. This would have prevented plant growth and caused temperatures to drop significantly.

A large asteroid impact likely killed off the dinosaurs.

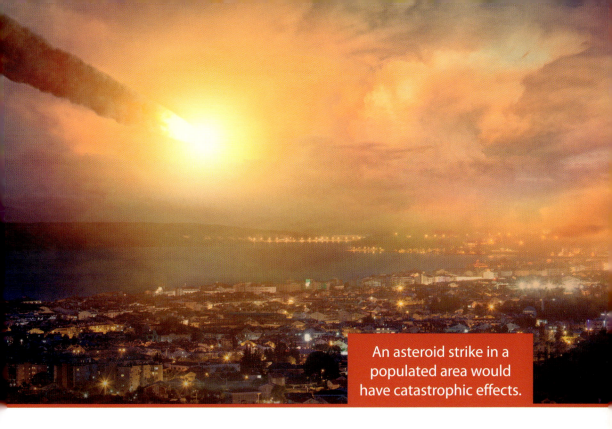

An asteroid strike in a populated area would have catastrophic effects.

Large meteorites are rare, but the risk of a devastating strike still exists. In 2013, a bright meteor sped over Russia at more than 11 miles (18 km) per second and exploded just 14 miles (23 km) overhead. It blew out window glass for more than 200 square miles (518 sq km), injuring more than 1,000 people. The asteroid that caused this was about the size of a six-story building. By contrast, scientists estimate that the object that killed off the dinosaurs was between 4.4 and 6.2 miles (7 to 10 km) wide.

A driver's dashboard camera caught the exploding meteorite over Russia in 2013.

FEAR OF FALLING OBJECTS

Since Earth-damaging meteorites are possible, scientists watch closely for near-Earth objects (NEOs) and potentially hazardous asteroids (PHAs). NEOs are objects that are closer to Earth than 121 million miles (195 million km). PHAs are asteroids that are more than about 500 feet (150 m) wide and come closer than 4.7 million miles (7.5 million km). NASA's NEO observation program follows these objects with telescopes placed around the world. The telescopes let scientists track NEO orbits and sizes, assessing the potential risk of impact.

NASA's *WISE* spacecraft has helped search for many potentially hazardous asteroids.

Scientists are studying ways to stop hazardous asteroids before it's too late.

The dinosaurs had no way of knowing an asteroid was coming or how to prevent the impact. Human scientists can detect incoming bodies and are developing ways to avoid a disaster. Since scientists can predict when and where a meteorite might land, evacuating the impact zone is one approach. Another solution is attempting to blow up the asteroid with nuclear weapons. However, scientists would also need to ensure the resulting pieces were too small to do damage.

A less risky idea is to gently redirect the object's orbit before it enters Earth's atmosphere. This could be done by sending a spacecraft near the asteroid. The craft's tiny force of gravity would slightly shift the object's path. This is a slow solution, though. It could take up to a century to nudge the object out of its orbit. Another approach is to knock an asteroid off course more forcefully.

NASA is working to test this last idea. Working with other agencies, it created the *Double Asteroid Redirection Test* (*DART*) mission. In November 2021, NASA launched a spacecraft

Crashing a spacecraft into an asteroid is one way to change the asteroid's course.

Engineers prepared the *DART* spacecraft for launch in late 2021.

specially made to crash into Dimorphos, a tiny body that orbits the asteroid Didymos, and change its orbit. The asteroid is not a threat to Earth. But if the test succeeded, scientists would know that shifting a threatening object's orbit is possible.

ASTEROIDS, COMETS, AND METEOROIDS

FAMOUS ASTEROIDS AND COMETS

About 329 miles (530 km) wide, Vesta is the largest known asteroid. It was discovered in 1807 and named for a Roman goddess. Vesta almost qualifies as a dwarf planet, but it is not quite a sphere. Its rocky surface is carved with a crater bigger than Earth's Grand Canyon. The asteroid is believed to have had water when it was young. Now it may have ice buried under its surface. Fragments of the asteroid that fell to Earth as meteorites helped scientists unlock some of Vesta's mysteries. Scientists learned a great deal more when the spacecraft *Dawn* orbited Vesta in 2011.

Sensors aboard *Dawn* detected hydrogen on Vesta, with the highest concentrations shown in red in this image.

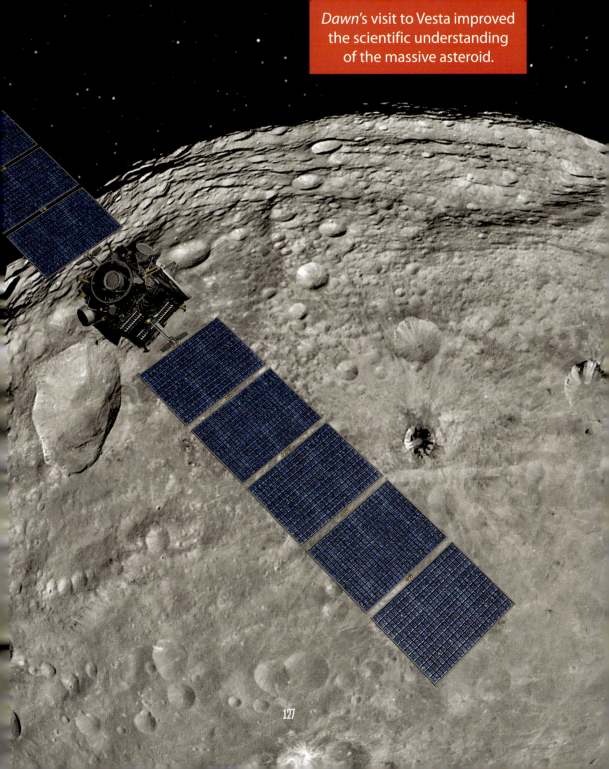

Dawn's visit to Vesta improved the scientific understanding of the massive asteroid.

ASTEROIDS, COMETS, AND METEOROIDS

News of the most famous comet was published in 1705 by British scientist Edmond Halley. He had studied historical accounts of comets appearing in the sky. Among the 24 comets he noted between 1337 and 1698, sightings in 1531, 1607, and 1682 were so much alike that he reasoned they must have been the same comet reappearing. It would next appear in 1758, he predicted. It did, and the comet was named Halley's Comet. This comet comes near Earth roughly every 75 years. It last appeared in 1986, and it is due to appear again in 2061.

An illustration of the 1835 appearance of Halley's Comet

The spacecraft *Giotto* observed Halley's Comet up close.

When Halley's Comet appeared in 1986, the Soviet Union and France worked together to launch spacecraft for the first close-up view. The ESA, Japan, and the United States also sent missions to study the comet. The spacecraft returned valuable photos and data to Earth. Even though the comet appears rarely, the debris it leaves behind causes meteor showers every year. The Orionid shower occurs every October, and the Eta Aquarids happen each May.

ASTEROIDS, COMETS, AND METEOROIDS

Astronauts took photos of Hale-Bopp from orbit in 1997.

A more recent discovery was the Hale-Bopp Comet in 1995. Professional astronomer Alan Hale and amateur astronomer Thomas Bopp each discovered it independently on the same night. Most comets have centers, or nuclei, roughly 1 to 2 miles (1.6 to 3.2 km) wide. Hale-Bopp's is believed to be about 25 miles (40 km) wide. This makes it appear very bright in the sky. It could be seen with the naked eye for 18 months, which was a record. Comets usually have two tails. One is a dust tail, lit by the sun, and the other is a tail of charged atoms. In 1997, by using a powerful telescope, European astronomers found Hale-Bopp had a third tail. This one is made of the element sodium and stretches for some 31 million miles (about 50 million km). Hale-Bopp's last visit past Earth was thousands of years before the 1995 appearance. Astronomers expect the comet to return in the year 4385.

NASA believes that billions of comets likely exist in the solar system. It has identified just a few thousand. The number of asteroids may total about four million. Astronomers have catalogued about one million of them. Each year, dozens of comets and thousands of asteroids are discovered.

NASA astronomers took a photo of the comet ISON from Earth in November 2013.

STARS

The stars were important to many ancient civilizations.

Ancient cultures had a variety of beliefs about the dots of light they saw in the night sky. Early Hebrews believed that the stars danced to delight the first man, Adam, in paradise. For the Maoris of New Zealand, stars were the souls of heroes. The brightest stars had killed the most enemies in battle. For the Chaldeans of Babylonia, they were lamps hanging from strings, and the angels watched over them. The stars have always been a source of wonder to people. Many worshipped them or thought they marked a path to the next life.

People also discovered that the stars had practical uses. They learned to use the stars to tell them when to plant, how to navigate over land and sea, and how to predict annual events like the flooding of the Nile River. They used the stars to create calendars. Some created buildings to face certain stars.

The buildings of the Inca people have been linked to the movements of the sun and other stars.

STARS

A STAR IS BORN

Stars are hot, glowing spheres of gas. They form mainly from clouds of gas and dust during the birth of their solar systems. Scientists have witnessed the star-making process thanks to the Hubble Space Telescope. The telescope has observed an area of space with a massive protostar, which is a young, growing star. The rare massive protostars created in this area are known as B-type stars. Five times hotter than the sun, these blue-white stars are nearly the hottest in the galaxy. Scientists were interested in the way such protostars shoot streams of

New stars are born in vast regions of gas and dust.

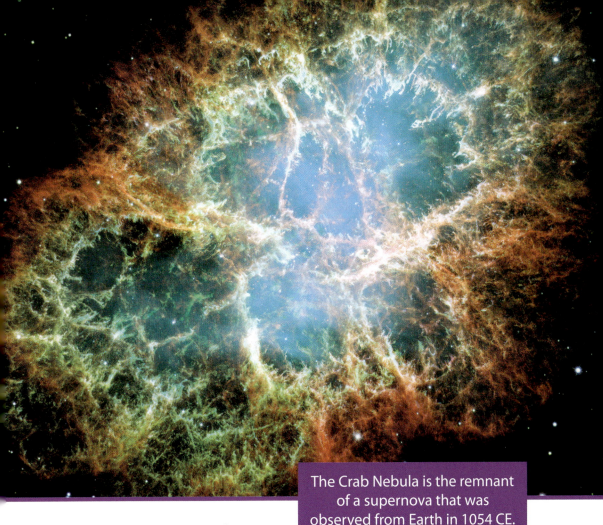

The Crab Nebula is the remnant of a supernova that was observed from Earth in 1054 CE.

bright gas into space. They knew the gas streams played a role in creating smaller stars but wondered if they worked the same way with rarer massive stars. Hubble, together with another type of telescope, showed them that the process is the same.

 The death of a star is closely tied with the birth of new stars. Certain massive stars end their lives as supernovae. These massive explosions release a star's remaining matter outward into space. Those materials then become part of new stars that are beginning to form.

STARS

A space telescope captured this view of multiple stars being born.

STARS OF MANY COLORS

Some potential stars never light up. Called brown dwarfs or failed stars, they aren't big enough for their cores to reach the pressures and temperatures needed to trigger nuclear fusion. This is a state in which hydrogen atoms fuse together to form helium atoms, releasing massive amounts of energy. When this process begins, the object fits the definition of a star.

Stars come in many sizes, temperatures, and colors. Most are red dwarf stars, the smallest type. These are invisible to people on Earth without a telescope. They burn only a little hydrogen in their cores. Orange and yellow-white stars are larger than red dwarfs and smaller than white stars like Earth's sun. There are also blue-white and blue-violet stars. Stars in this last category are rare, giant, and the hottest of all stars. They are also the easiest to see without a telescope.

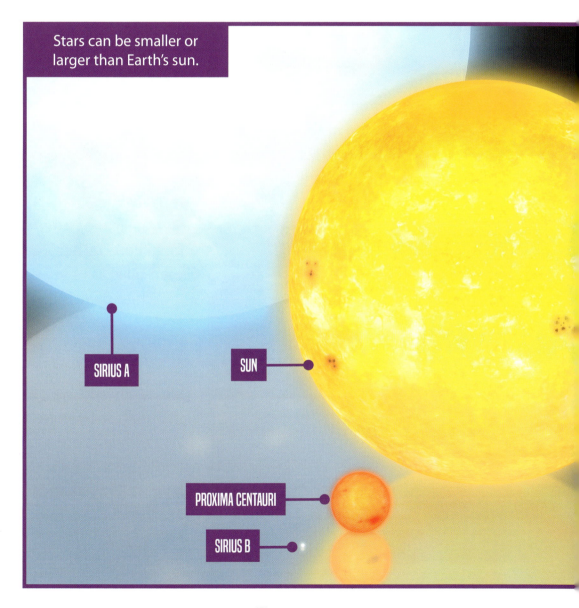

Stars can be smaller or larger than Earth's sun.

STARS

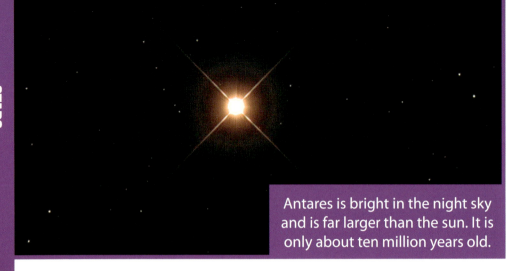

Antares is bright in the night sky and is far larger than the sun. It is only about ten million years old.

Scientists categorize stars in their type and life cycle on a track known as the main sequence. As they grow older, the stars travel up the track, turning brighter and bluer over billions of years. The bigger the star, the shorter its life span. A short-lived star's lifetime is measured in millions rather than billions of years.

White dwarfs and neutron stars have completed the main part of their life cycles and are off the main sequence. White dwarfs are the cores of stars that have collapsed and are dying. Stars that are medium-size and smaller die

An image from NASA's *Galaxy Evolution Explorer* spacecraft shows the formation of a white dwarf in the Helix Nebula.

A NASA illustration shows a comet being drawn in by a white dwarf's powerful gravity.

this way. While they can still be very hot, they give off little light. Since most stars are medium-size or smaller, most will become white dwarfs one day. Because they are so dense, white dwarfs have enormously strong gravity. At 350,000 times stronger than Earth's gravity, a white dwarf's gravity would make a 150-pound (68 kg) person standing on the star weigh 50 million pounds (23 million kg).

STARS

A neutron star is one of the densest objects in the universe.

Neutron stars are similar, except that they are the remnants of more massive stars. They have used up their fuel, and their core is collapsing. A white dwarf can be 600 times wider than a neutron star. But the neutron star has about 400,000 times stronger gravity and magnetic force. Neutron stars are hotter at birth and spin faster. They are created during a supernova.

A core that was once 5,000 miles (8,000 km) wide can shrink to 12 miles (19 km) wide. A piece of a neutron star the size of a sugar cube would weigh about 2.2 trillion pounds (1 trillion kg) on Earth.

An illustration shows the violent merger of two neutron stars.

STARS

Black holes are among the most mysterious and fascinating structures in space.

Some supernovas create black holes instead of neutron stars. This happens when a dying star is especially large. Stripped of the star's outer layers, the tightly packed inner layers are all that remains of the star. A tremendous amount of mass is compressed into a tiny area.

Scientists learn about black holes by observing how they affect the area around them. Their gravity is very strong, drawing in whatever is nearby. For example, if a star passes by a black hole, it will be torn apart as the black hole draws it in. Even light cannot escape the pull of a black hole's gravity. Scientists believe the Milky Way galaxy may have up to a billion black holes. A gigantic black hole called Sagittarius A* is located at the galaxy's center.

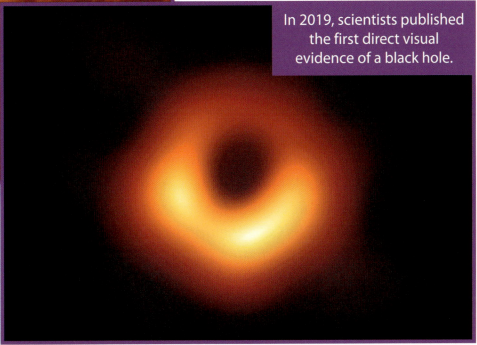

In 2019, scientists published the first direct visual evidence of a black hole.

STARS

Constellations are linked to important parts of mythologies from around the world.

CONSTELLATIONS

For thousands of years, people have observed the stars and connected them with invisible lines to form pictures. France has cave paintings of stars dating back 17,000 years. People of many cultures saw patterns in the sky and linked them to their own myths and legends. These patterns are known as constellations.

Today, people recognize constellations developed by ancient Greek and Babylonian astronomers. The Persian astronomer Abd al-Rahman al-Sufi produced a book of constellations in the 900s CE. It included both Greek and Arabic constellations. Modern international groups of astronomers have officially designated 88 distinct constellations in the night sky.

Orion, the hunter, is one notable constellation from Greek mythology.

STARS

The Southern Cross has long had a practical use for navigation in the Southern Hemisphere.

Other star pictures, called asterisms, are separate from traditional constellations and much newer. The Southern Cross, for example, is seen in the Southern Hemisphere. It has five stars contained within Crux, the smallest constellation. Four of the stars are very bright. With the longer part of the cross pointing toward the South Pole, it is a guide to travelers on land and sea. European explorers named it in the 1500s. The Southern Cross is featured on the flags

The flag of Australia

of five countries: New Zealand, Australia, Samoa, Papua New Guinea, and Brazil.

The Big Dipper is another well-known asterism. It is composed of seven stars all within the constellation Ursa Major. This set of stars suggests different images and names in different cultures. In Africa, it has been called the Drinking Gourd. Enslaved people in the American South passed along that image from their homeland. Those who were escaping to freedom in the North were often advised to follow the Drinking Gourd. This helped them locate the North Star, also called Polaris, over the North Pole. At the end of the Big Dipper are two stars that point to the end of the handle of another asterism, the Little Dipper. There sits the North Star, pointing to true north.

The Big Dipper is easy to locate on a clear night.

STARS

NOTABLE STARS

Thanks to the motion of Earth's axis over time, the star that indicates north shifts from the perspective of those on the planet. Thousands of years ago, the star Vega was the North Star. Vega, a bright star that is part of the constellation Lyra, is expected to return to its North Star role in about 12,000 years.

Like the current North Star, Vega is big and bright. It's also fast. It rotates on its axis at 170 miles (274 km) per second. This causes the star to bulge outward in the middle. Its temperature is lower at its poles than around the middle because it is not as round as most stars.

One of the largest known stars, UY Scuti, is known as a hypergiant. The star's size increases and decreases over time, making it tricky to get a precise measurement. But it's believed

Vega is bright and has a blue color.

to be 1,700 times as wide as the sun. If it were put in the sun's place, the star's edges would extend past Jupiter's orbit. Such hypergiant stars are in the late stages of their lives.

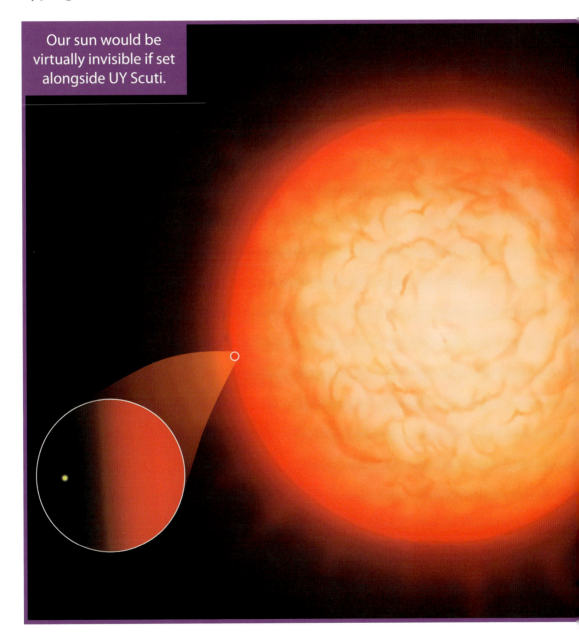

Our sun would be virtually invisible if set alongside UY Scuti.

GALAXIES

A river of stars in the night sky is evidence of Earth's place in the Milky Way galaxy.

A huge mass of smudgy-looking stars seems to flow down the night sky like a celestial river. People in ancient China called it the Silver River. They believed this sky river kept the goddess represented by the star Vega from her human love, represented by the star Altair. Some people in Africa saw it as campfire ashes, while some in Polynesia saw it as a big, blue, cloud-eating shark. The ancient Greeks called it the Milky Way after a myth about spilled milk. Today, this is still its common name.

Scientists have since learned that this collection of stars is part of our own galaxy. It is Earth's view outward from inside a galaxy containing billions of stars. The Milky Way galaxy is home to not only Earth's solar system but also many billions of other stars and planets. Gravity is the glue that holds everything together.

A galaxy called NGC 6744 has a structure similar to the Milky Way.

GALAXIES

THE EARLY GALAXY

The European spacecraft *Gaia* collected data about the Milky Way's history in the 2010s. *Gaia* analyzed the positions and brightness of more than one billion stars. The resulting data suggested that the Milky Way's history is much more active and violent than previously thought.

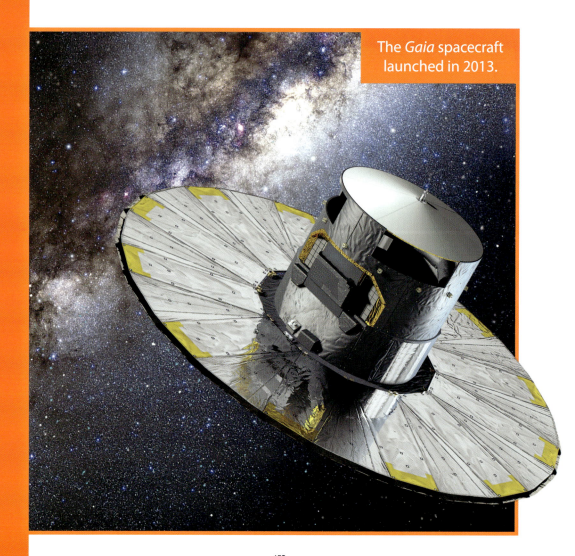

The *Gaia* spacecraft launched in 2013.

Gaia peered deep into the galaxy's history.

Gaia found unexpectedly old stars in the main disc of the Milky Way. Computer simulations suggested that some of these stars may have existed before the galaxy formed. They were born in clouds of gas and dust nearby. Then gravitational forces brought them into the forming Milky Way.

Studying ancient stars has helped scientists better understand the history of our galaxy.

GALAXIES

Gaia also found evidence of collisions in the Milky Way's past. The spacecraft detected a collection of stars moving around the galactic center in a way that suggested they had come from a single, separate place. Astronomers believe the Milky Way and a dwarf galaxy called Gaia-Enceladus crashed into each other about ten billion years ago. This slow-motion crash would have taken place over millions of years. The Milky Way absorbed the other galaxy, adding the stars to its own.

Scientists have observed galactic collisions through telescopes.

Scientists suspect there have been at least 12 such crashes in the Milky Way's lifetime. They are still sorting out how many there were and what objects were involved. Another collision scientists discovered was with a galaxy they called Kraken. Taking place 11 billion years ago, it was likely the biggest crash of all. At the time, the Milky Way was one-fourth of its current mass. Thirteen large clusters of ancient stars that are still part of the galaxy today may have come from the encounter with Kraken.

The galaxy NGC 6052 was once thought to be a single unusual galaxy. Scientists later determined it is actually a new galaxy in the process of forming from the merger of two other galaxies.

GALAXIES

THE SIZE AND SHAPE OF THE MILKY WAY

To deal with space's vast size, astronomers often measure distance in terms of light-years. One light-year equals the distance light travels in space in a year. It is equivalent to about 5.88 trillion miles (9.46 trillion km). The Milky Way is

An artist's depiction shows what scientists believe the Milky Way galaxy looks like from afar.

The Sombrero Galaxy is a spiral galaxy that appears nearly edge-on when observed from Earth.

about 100,000 light-years across and 1,000 light-years thick. A bulge at the center, which holds old stars, is about 10,000 light-years wide.

Like many other galaxies, the Milky Way has a spiral shape with four arms stretching out from it. Earth's solar system sits on the Orion Arm, one of the two smaller arms. The arms are not permanent. They form and drift apart over spans of millions of years. The arms are filled with stars of various ages and sizes, plus the dust and gas needed to form more. Spiral galaxies have a bulge at the center and a disk of gas and stars around it. Some scientists describe them as looking like fried eggs. Because of the disk, they're often called disk galaxies.

GALAXIES

Scientists have observed a supermassive black hole at the center of the galaxy NGC 4845.

Scientists have also long believed that a supermassive black hole sits in the bulge. It has become known as Sagittarius A*. The stars in that area race around the black hole, which suggests its enormous size. Scientists estimate that it has a mass about 3.7 million times greater than that of the sun.

The Milky Way is part of what is known as the Local Group. This is a collection of some 40 galaxies held together by gravity. The Andromeda Galaxy, another galaxy with a spiral shape, is the other large player in the group. It is relatively close to the Milky Way and is clearly visible from Earth on a dark night. Most of the other galaxies in the Local Group are small dwarf galaxies. With as few as 100 million stars each, they have relatively little light and tend to be found in clusters. Membership in the Local Group changes gradually as galaxies merge with one another. The Local Group is near a large cluster of galaxies called the Virgo cluster. It is believed to have about 2,000 galaxies. Scientists expect that the Local Group may one day join the Virgo cluster.

The Andromeda Galaxy is one of the nearest large neighbors to the Milky Way.

GALAXIES

GALAXY DIVERSITY

Most of the galaxies near the Milky Way are spiral galaxies with flat, bluish disks of stars. They are the easiest galaxies to spot. Two other major types are elliptical and irregular. All three come in various sizes, ranging from dwarf to giant galaxies. A giant galaxy can include trillions of stars.

NGC 3610 is an example of an elliptical galaxy.

Elliptical galaxies are oval in shape. Some are almost circular, while others are stretched out in a wide ellipse. About a third of all galaxies are elliptical. With little dust and gas, they no longer build new stars. Most ellipticals are dwarfs. They tend to be only a few thousand light-years wide. But the largest galaxies are ellipticals. A giant elliptical galaxy called IC 1101 is the largest known elliptical galaxy. It is part of the Virgo cluster. At 5.8 million light-years wide, it is 50 times wider than the Milky Way. Astronomers estimate it contains 100 trillion stars. Scientists think colliding, combining galaxies may have resulted in the enormous sizes of many of these galaxies.

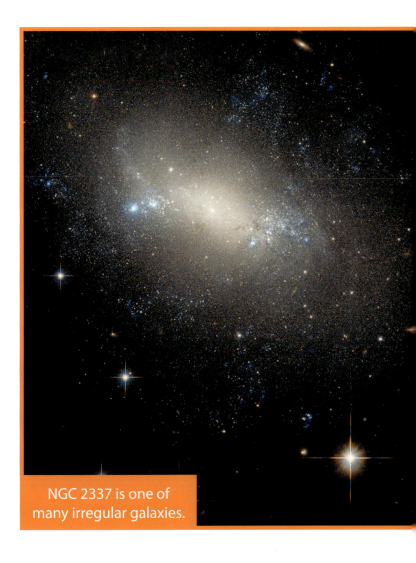

NGC 2337 is one of many irregular galaxies.

GALAXIES

Crashes are responsible for irregular galaxies. Their shapes can also come from chaotic collisions within themselves. Irregular galaxies may simply be affected by the gravity of nearby galaxies. These galaxies don't fit into one of the other types. They usually have young and old stars, along with the gas and dust to make more. However, they are not as bright as spiral galaxies. The Large and Small Magellanic Clouds, companions of the Milky Way, are well-known examples of irregular galaxies. Both orbit the Milky Way every 1.5 billion years. Every 900 million years, they complete an orbit around each other.

The Large and Small Magellanic Clouds can be seen under very dark conditions.

PGC 83677 is a lenticular galaxy.

Lenticular galaxies are a cross between an elliptical and a spiral galaxy. They have the bulges and disks of spiral galaxies but lack the spiral's arms. These galaxies come not from crashes but from spiral galaxies running out of gas. They can't create new stars. Instead, the existing stars pull on each other with their own gravity. This causes the galaxies to look a bit elliptical, even though their disks rotate. Viewed from the side, they are thin at the edge and thicker toward the middle. The galaxy NGC 5010 is an example of a lenticular galaxy. It is located in the Virgo constellation about 140 million light-years from Earth.

GALAXIES

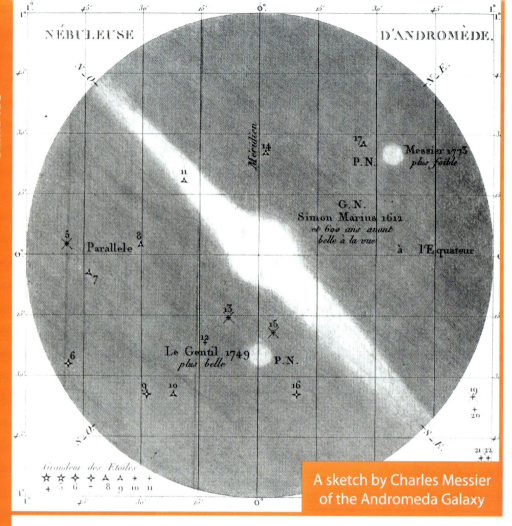

A sketch by Charles Messier of the Andromeda Galaxy

DISCOVERING MORE GALAXIES

The Milky Way galaxy was once thought to contain everything in space. But this turned out to be an Earth-centered view. Discoveries over time hinted that there might be more to the universe. In the 1700s, French astronomer Charles Messier saw many smudgy objects in the sky. His goal was to find comets. These other smudgy objects could be confused for comets, so he made a list of them to avoid a mix-up. At that time, objects like this were called nebulae. Some of them had a spiral shape when viewed through a telescope.

In 1924, American astronomer Edwin Hubble showed that most of those spiral nebulae were too far away to be part of the Milky Way. Suddenly the universe became much larger. The Milky Way was just one among an enormous sea of galaxies. Scientists now define the term *nebula* as a huge dust and gas cloud in space in which stars can be formed.

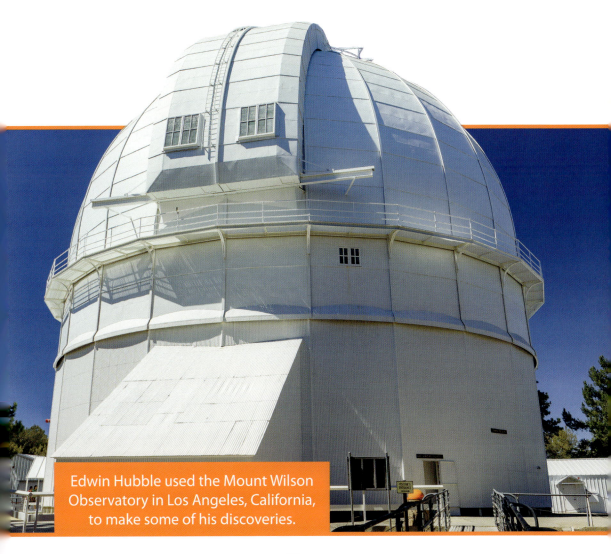

Edwin Hubble used the Mount Wilson Observatory in Los Angeles, California, to make some of his discoveries.

GALAXIES

The two Magellanic Clouds, both irregular dwarf galaxies, are found in the skies of the Southern Hemisphere, where they have guided many sailors traveling those oceans. The Large Magellanic Cloud contains approximately 30 billion stars, while the Small Magellanic Cloud has about three billion. The Clouds'

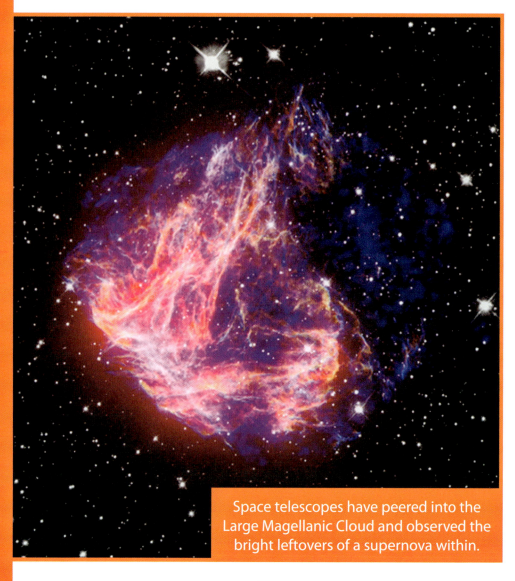

Space telescopes have peered into the Large Magellanic Cloud and observed the bright leftovers of a supernova within.

Triangulum is large and bright enough to be viewed by amateur astronomers using backyard telescopes.

closeness to the gravity of the Milky Way may account for their irregular shapes. They are part of the Local Group of galaxies.

Another member of the Local Group is Triangulum, the third largest galaxy in the area after Andromeda and the Milky Way. A spiral galaxy, its name comes from the constellation Triangulum. It is nicknamed the Pinwheel Galaxy because of the way it looks like a pinwheel from the view of the Milky Way. At 60,000 light-years across, Triangulum is about 60 percent of the width of the Milky Way and contains about 40 billion stars. Scientists discovered that Triangulum is moving toward Andromeda and may be in the process of a long orbit around it.

GALAXIES

THE ANDROMEDA COLLISION

Only a few galaxies can be seen without a telescope. Andromeda is one of them. At about 2.5 million light-years away, the Andromeda Galaxy is the Milky Way's closest large neighbor. This spiral galaxy is larger than the Milky Way, stretching about 200,000 light-years across compared with the Milky Way's 100,000. It may have twice the number of stars as the Milky Way.

Andromeda will grow larger and larger in Earth's night sky as it approaches the Milky Way.

The effects of gravity will distort the appearance of the two galaxies as they grow nearer.

    Scientists have long known that Andromeda is on a collision course with the Milky Way. Research shows that this collision may have already begun. Many galaxies, including Andromeda and the Milky Way, have a halo of gas, dust, and a few stars surrounding them. Scientists realized that Andromeda's halo stretches far beyond the galaxy. It reaches about half the distance to the Milky Way. While it's difficult for scientists to measure the Milky Way's halo, they believe it's probably similar to Andromeda's. If so, the two halos could already be touching.

    Scientists estimate that the Andromeda Galaxy is moving toward the Milky Way at about 68 miles (110 km) per second. Andromeda will grow larger and larger in the sky until finally colliding with the Milky Way in about 4.5 billion years. The two galaxies will circle around each other before settling to form a single combined galaxy about ten billion years from now. Because the galaxies are made up mostly of the empty space between stars, the chance of any objects in the two galaxies actually colliding is extremely small.

GALAXIES

GALAXY CLUSTERS

Even bigger than galaxies are galaxy clusters, groups of two or more galaxies held together by gravity. Some clusters contain thousands of galaxies. The Milky Way's Local Group is a galaxy cluster. Another example, one of the largest known, is El Gordo. Its name means "the fat one" in Spanish. It is estimated to contain about 3,000 times the mass of the Milky Way. Discovered in 2012, El Gordo is really two galaxy clusters in the process of combining.

A galaxy cluster called Abell 370 contains hundreds of galaxies.

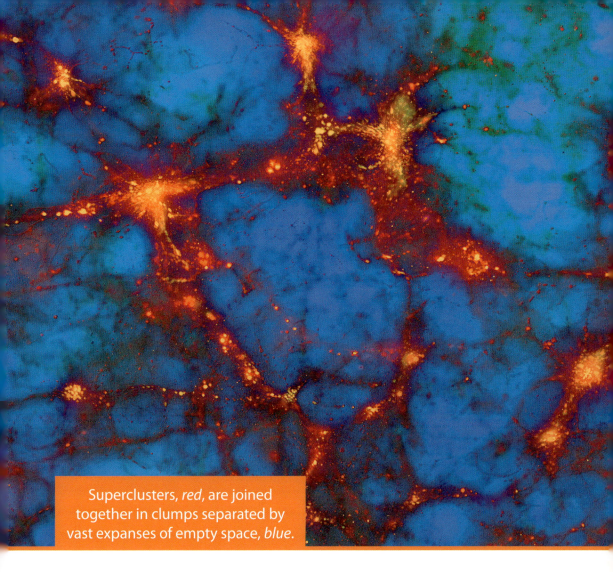

Superclusters, *red*, are joined together in clumps separated by vast expanses of empty space, *blue*.

Even bigger than El Gordo, though, are superclusters. These form when gravity joins multiple galaxy clusters together. Perhaps the largest known supercluster is Vela, discovered in 2016. One member of the team that found it, Professor Matthew Colless, says it may contain 100,000 galaxies. Its gravity is pulling on the Milky Way, despite Vela being some 840 million light-years from Earth. The Milky Way may one day become part of the Vela supercluster, but if so, that day is five trillion years in the future.

THE UNIVERSE

The universe includes everything in existence, ranging from giant objects such as galaxy clusters to the tiniest particles that make up individual atoms. Stars, planets, moons, asteroids, comets, and black holes are part of the universe. So are living creatures on Earth. Our planet is one among countless worlds in the universe.

It can be hard to imagine the sheer scale of the universe.

A nearly limitless number of unknown stars, planets, moons, and other objects fills the universe.

THE BIG BANG

One of the greatest mysteries of the universe is how it came into being. Most scientists believe the Big Bang theory is the likeliest explanation. In this theory, the universe began about 13.8 billion years ago as an extremely hot, dense ball of matter. Science writer David J. Eicher notes that the question of what created that ball of matter "is outside the realm of science because it can't be answered by scientific means." Scientists are more concerned with piecing together how the universe formed after that point.

Determining what happened in the universe's first few moments is extremely challenging.

Once elements like hydrogen appeared in the universe, stars were able to form.

The term *Big Bang* refers to the sudden, rapid, enormous expansion of that ball of matter. This explosion brought matter, energy, space, and time into existence. Within a second of the Big Bang, the universe cooled enough for protons, electrons, and neutrons to form. These are the building blocks that make up atoms of matter. However, the intense heat and radiation of the early universe prevented these particles from joining together to actually form atoms. About 400,000 years after the Big Bang, the continued cooling of the universe allowed electrons to join with protons to form the element hydrogen.

THE UNIVERSE

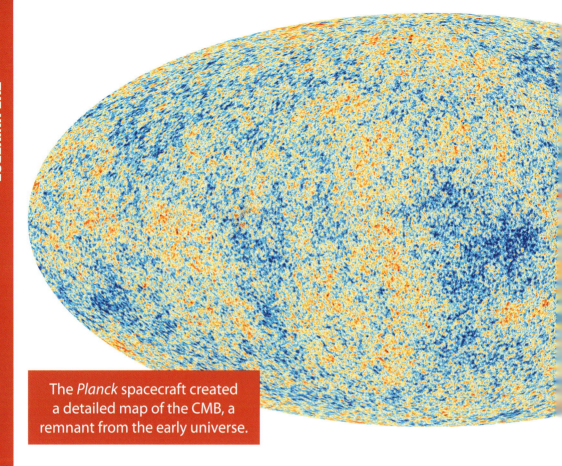

The *Planck* spacecraft created a detailed map of the CMB, a remnant from the early universe.

THE OBSERVABLE UNIVERSE

Scientists have detected radiation left over from the Big Bang. This radiation is known as the cosmic microwave background (CMB). At the time atoms were able to form, matter became separate from radiation. The echoes of this event are the CMB. A map of the CMB created by the European Space Agency's *Planck* spacecraft revealed that the universe is about 13.8 billion years old.

Because light moves at a set speed, this means we can see about 13.8 billion light-years in each direction. Astronomers can detect only light that has had time to reach Earth. This region that scientists can study is known as the observable universe. Because the universe continues to expand, the exact size of the observable universe is uncertain. Scientists do not know what lies beyond the boundaries of the observable universe.

Until the 1990s, scientists thought that the expansion of the universe was slowing down over time. They believed that the force of gravity would pull the universe's objects back together. However, the Hubble Space Telescope's observations of distant objects revealed that the expansion in the past was slower than it is today. This means the universe's expansion is actually speeding up.

The expansion of the universe is driving objects in space farther apart.

THE UNIVERSE

DARK ENERGY AND DARK MATTER

Researchers searched for an explanation for the accelerated expansion. They came up with a concept that could explain what they were seeing. They called it dark energy. Scientists determined that about 68 percent of the universe is made up of dark energy. Still, they are uncertain about what it is or how it works.

The true nature of dark energy is one of the universe's most puzzling mysteries.

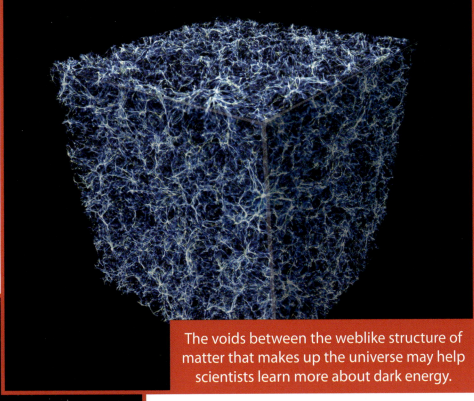

The voids between the weblike structure of matter that makes up the universe may help scientists learn more about dark energy.

In late 2021, scientists announced they had found a supervoid located in a constellation called Eridanus. A supervoid is a huge area where matter is widely spread. In other words, it's a low-density area. This results in a large, cold region. The universe is already quite cold, but this area is much colder than it is elsewhere. The cold is only partly explained by the supervoid. Scientists think dark energy may be involved, too. Much is yet to be learned about this newly discovered spot, but astronomers are hopeful that it will teach them more about dark energy.

THE UNIVERSE

The distortion of galaxies in the cluster Abell 1689 hints at the force of gravity caused in part by dark matter, *highlighted purple*.

About 27 percent of the universe is made up of what scientists call dark matter. Dark matter is not related to dark energy other than being another unknown element in the universe. Scientists know a little bit about it by ruling out what it is not. It isn't visible. It isn't composed of the same material as stars and planets. It does not include black holes. It doesn't give off any of the X-rays or radio waves that other objects in space do.

Scientists know dark matter is there because its gravity affects galaxies. Even in the late 1800s, astronomers could tell from their observations that some unseen source of gravity had to be at work in the universe. In 1933, astronomer Fritz Zwicky reported that faraway galaxies were orbiting faster than their mass would seem to allow. Few paid attention to Zwicky's findings until the 1970s, when astronomers Kent Ford and Vera Rubin saw the same thing happening with stars in the Andromeda Galaxy. Finally, scientists started seeing this everywhere.

Fritz Zwicky helped lay the groundwork for today's understanding of dark matter.

THE UNIVERSE

An astronaut on a space walk works on a device meant to detect dark matter.

Most scientists think dark matter is made of particles that act differently than known particles. Some call them Weakly Interacting Massive Particles (WIMPs). They are weak because their effects on normal matter are limited. No one yet has found a WIMP, though they have tried. Some scientists suspect they aren't real. Some feel that the extra-fast orbits are the result of other effects of gravity.

Just 5 percent of the universe is made up of normal matter. This includes all the galaxies, stars, and planets in Earth's

182

night sky. It includes all known life. Working to unlock the secrets of the remaining 95 percent of the universe is one of the most exciting puzzles in science.

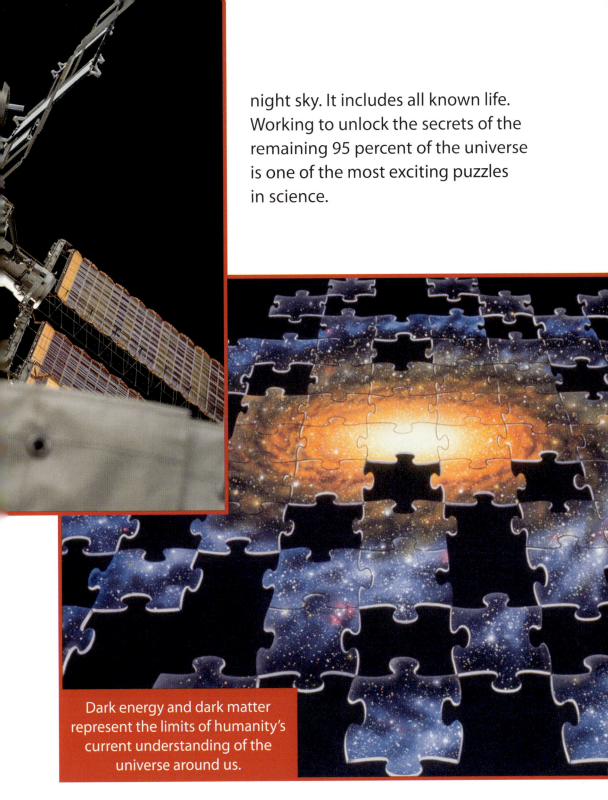

Dark energy and dark matter represent the limits of humanity's current understanding of the universe around us.

183

THE UNIVERSE

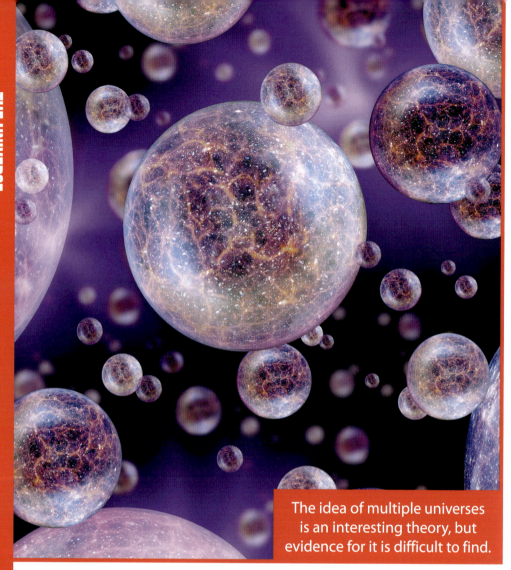

The idea of multiple universes is an interesting theory, but evidence for it is difficult to find.

THE MULTIVERSE?

Scientists now estimate that the universe has 100 billion galaxies. Everything we know is contained within the universe. But could there be more than one universe? What if our universe is just one of many? Some scientists think this could be the case. This concept is known as the multiverse.

Believers in multiple universes have different ideas of what they might be. The basis of the idea is that the period of wild inflation following the Big Bang didn't end all at once in every spot. Some areas might have created more universes. Each might operate differently and contain different sorts of particles.

Arizona State University scientist Heling Deng is looking to certain black holes for evidence. A multiverse theory expert, Deng thinks that as a new universe grows, it may divide into two or more. There would be signs of that division left behind. Certain types of black holes might be that sign. So far, no definitive evidence of other universes has been found.

The concept of multiple similar universes is a common theme in science fiction.

CONCLUSION

Amazing new advances in the study of space are on the horizon. NASA has studied distant galaxies with powerful space telescopes, but many unanswered questions about our universe remain. Some of those questions may be answered by the James Webb Space Telescope. This deep-space telescope, more powerful than Hubble, launched in late 2021. It will look into the universe's distant past and study exoplanets orbiting faraway stars.

The main mirror of the James Webb Space Telescope is enormous.

NASA has sent spacecraft to all the planets in our solar system, but our neighborhood in space still holds many mysteries. A new generation of robotic spacecraft will travel to Jupiter's moon Europa, the planet Venus, and the sun, improving our understanding of the solar system. In one ambitious mission, the planned *Dragonfly* spacecraft will land on Saturn's moon Titan in the 2030s. It will then use rotors to fly from place to place on the intriguing moon.

Closer to home, the technology of human space exploration is making important strides. Reusable rockets are helping lower the cost of space travel. Space agencies are seeking to send astronauts back to the moon. In the longer term, engineers are beginning to develop plans for human landings on Mars.

The human understanding of space has come a long way since ancient people first looked up at the night sky. From telescopes to rockets to robotic spacecraft, new technologies have helped astronomers unlock many of the universe's secrets. Today, the next generation of scientists is building on this legacy to improve our understanding of space.

The first human landings on Mars will likely be within the lifetimes of people living today.

GLOSSARY

carbon dioxide
A colorless gas made of one part carbon and two parts oxygen.

celestial
In or related to outer space.

cosmic
Related to the universe.

counterclockwise
Moving in the opposite direction as the hands of a clock.

galactic
Related to one or more galaxies.

helium
A colorless, odorless gas that is lighter than air.

hormone
A natural chemical in the body.

hydrogen
A colorless, odorless gas that burns very easily and forms water when combined with oxygen. The most common element in the universe.

microwave
A type of electromagnetic wave.

molecule
The smallest particle of a substance, composed of two or more atoms.

satellite
A natural or human-made object that orbits a larger body.

sphere
A globe or ball shape.

TO LEARN MORE

FURTHER READINGS

Hubbard, Ben. *The Complete Guide to Space Exploration*. Lonely Planet Kids, 2020.

Hulick, Kathryn. *The Night Sky*. Abdo, 2022.

Space: A Visual Encyclopedia. DK, 2020.

ONLINE RESOURCES

To learn more about space, please visit **abdobooklinks.com** or scan this QR code. These links are routinely monitored and updated to provide the most current information available.

INDEX

Armstrong, Neil, 86
asteroid belt, 55, 114
asteroids, 6, 13, 46, 112–114, 116–118, 120–126, 131, 172
astronauts, 84–86, 96, 99, 101, 103–106, 187
astronomers, 10, 45, 47, 52, 55, 56, 130–131, 144, 154, 156, 161, 164–165, 176, 179, 181, 187
atmosphere, 5, 14, 20, 31, 38, 40–41, 42, 44, 50, 62, 69, 84, 88–89, 91, 94–95, 97, 99, 107, 116–119, 124
auroras, 30–31

Big Bang, 174–175, 176, 185
black holes, 142–143, 158, 172, 181, 185

comets, 6, 13, 46, 114–117, 128–129, 130–131, 164, 172
constellations, 144–148, 163, 167, 179
craters, 61–62, 119–120, 126

dark energy, 178–181
dark matter, 181–182
dwarf planets, 53–55, 126

Earth, 5–6, 8–9, 12, 18, 20, 25–28, 31, 35, 40–41, 64–67, 70–73, 101, 116, 118–119
exoplanets, 56–57, 186

Gagarin, Yuri, 84
galaxies, 7, 15, 134, 143, 150–171, 172, 181–182, 184, 186

Halley's Comet, 128–129

Jupiter, 34, 44–45, 55, 92, 114

Kuiper belt, 52, 55

light-years, 6–7, 156–157, 161, 163, 167–168, 171, 176
lunar eclipse, 58, 69

magnetic fields, 27, 41
Mars, 35, 42–43, 55, 90–91, 110, 114, 118, 187
Mercury, 35–36
meteorites, 112–113, 116–119, 121–123, 126
meteoroids, 41, 112–114, 116, 119
meteors, 116–117, 119, 121, 129
Milky Way, 7, 143, 150–154, 156–158, 160–162, 164–165, 167–171
moon landings, 86
moon phases, 58, 66–69, 72, 74
moons, 6–7, 13, 28, 36, 39, 41, 43, 45–47, 49, 51–52, 58–77, 84–86, 90, 94–95, 114, 118, 172, 186–187
multiverse, 184–185

NASA (National Aeronautics and Space Administration), 42, 56, 90–91, 94–95, 102–103, 106–107, 122, 124–125, 131, 186–187
nebulae, 16, 32, 164–165
Neptune, 7, 34, 50–51, 92

observable universe, 176–177

planets, 6–7, 8–9, 12–13, 15, 18, 32–57, 65, 71, 88–95, 112, 114, 151, 172, 182, 186–187
Pluto, 52–54

rockets, 78–80, 83–84, 86, 102, 104–111, 187
rovers, 42, 90–91

satellites, 82–83, 102–103
Saturn, 34, 46–47, 92, 94–95, 187
solar eclipse, 28–29
solar nebula, 16–17, 32
solar system, 6–7, 12–13, 32–55, 88–95, 114–115, 131, 134, 151, 157, 186
space exploration, 78–111, 186–187
Space Race, 82–86, 96–99
space stations, 96–101, 103
spacecraft, 7, 26–27, 38, 42, 49, 82–111, 124–126, 129, 152–154, 176, 186–187
Sputnik, 82–83
stars, 7, 12, 14, 16–19, 56–57, 112, 115, 132–149, 150–155, 157–163, 167–169, 172, 181–182, 186
sun, 6–7, 8–31, 32–33, 58, 66–68, 72–73, 130, 137, 186
supernovae, 16, 135, 140, 142

telescopes, 7, 55, 103–104, 122, 130, 134–137, 164, 168, 177, 186–187

universe, 7, 104, 164–165, 172–185, 186–187
Uranus, 34, 48–49, 92

Venus, 35, 38–39, 88–89, 186

PHOTO CREDITS

Cover Photos: NASA/JPL-Caltech/UCLA, front (Andromeda Galaxy); NASA, front (Earth, ISS), back (supernova); Marcel Clemens/Shutterstock, back (telescope); NASA/Johns Hopkins University APL/Carnegie Institution of Washington, front (Mercury); Vadim Sadovski/Shutterstock, front (comet); Shutterstock, front (space, Mars rover), back (rocket); Reid Wiseman/NASA, front (SpaceX Dragon); NASA Goddard, front (sun)

Interior Photos: Shutterstock, 2, 4, 6, 14, 15, 16–17, 18, 19, 24–25, 25, 30 (top), 37, 71, 72–73, 82, 94–95, 113, 116, 118–119, 121 (top), 132, 140, 144, 145, 147, 150, 153 (bottom), 162, 167, 174, 187; Vadim Sadovski/Shutterstock, 2–3; Mark Garlick/Science Source, 5, 61, 65, 137, 141, 149, 171, 177; John A. Davis/Shutterstock, 7; Mikkel Juul Jensen/Science Source, 8; Danny Ye/Shutterstock, 9; Everett/Shutterstock, 10–11, 81; KSC/JSC/NASA, 11; Lukasz Pawel Szczepanski/Shutterstock, 12, 175; Vladimir Arndt/Shutterstock, 13; JPL-Caltech/GSFC/NASA, 16; Valdis Skudre/Shutterstock, 20–21; Bear Fotos/Shutterstock, 21; Volodymyr Khytrykov/Shutterstock, 22; NASA/AP, 23; Leif Heimbold/KSC/NASA, 26; Johns Hopkins University APL/NASA, 27; Aubrey Gemignani/HQ/NASA, 28; Micha Weber/Shutterstock, 29; ESA/GSFC/NASA, 30 (bottom); JSC/NASA, 31, 60, 62–63, 64, 85 (top), 97, 98, 99 (bottom), 100, 103, 104, 105, 130, 182–183; Jurik Peter/Shutterstock, 32–33 (top), 114, 173, 178–179; Withan Tor/Shutterstock, 32–33 (bottom); JPL/NASA, 34, 38 (right), 39, 92, 93; ASU/MSSS/JPL-Caltech/NASA, 35; Carnegie Institution/Johns Hopkins University APL/JPL/NASA, 36; Hakan Akirmak Visuals/Shutterstock, 38 (left), 44; MSFC/NASA, 40, 78, 83, 84, 86, 157; Ann Stryzhekin/Shutterstock, 41; USGS/JPL/NASA, 42–43, 63; Pavel Gabzdyl/Shutterstock, 43; SETI Institute/JPL-Caltech/NASA, 45; SSI/JPL/NASA, 46–47, 47; JPL-Caltech/NASA, 48, 57, 91, 118, 122–123, 126–127, 142–143, 151, 156–157, 159; Lawrence Sromovsky/UW-Madison/W. W. Keck Observatory/JPL/NASA, 49; Voyager 2/JPL/NASA, 50; JPL/ARC/NASA, 51; SRI/Johns Hopkins University APL/JPL/NASA, 52, 54; STScI/ESA/JPL/NASA, 53, 134; UCLA/MPS/DLR/IDA/JPL-Caltech/NASA, 55; Daniel Rutter/Ames Research Center/NASA, 56; Fernando Astasio Avila/Shutterstock, 58; Lunar and Planetary Institute/NASA/Wikimedia, 59; Paolo G./Shutterstock, 66; Kathrine Andi/Shutterstock, 67; Sonia Prenneis/Shutterstock, 68; Marius Meyer/Shutterstock, 69; Sheila Terry/Science Source, 70; Bob Pool/Shutterstock, 73; Bronwyn Photo/Shutterstock, 74; Martin Fowler/Shutterstock, 75; Jean-Loup Charmet/Science Source, 76; Steve Sanchez/Shutterstock, 77; AP, 79, 80, 121 (bottom); Tass/AP, 85 (bottom); Apollo Lunar Surface Journal/NASA/Wikimedia, 87 (top); NASA/Wikimedia, 87 (bottom), 102; Detlev Van Ravensway/Science Source, 88, 89, 96, 120, 184; KSC/NASA/Wikimedia, 90; ESA/JPL/NASA, 95; Rob Griffith/AP, 99 (top); JSC/NASA/Wikimedia, 100–101; KSC/NASA/Wikimedia, 106–107; Bruce Weaver/AP, 107; Maxim Marmur/AP, 108; LM Otero/AP, 109; Space X/Wikimedia, 110–111; Inspiration 4/John Krauss/Cover Images/AP, 111; Science Source, 112; ESA/Rosetta/Osiris Team/Science Source, 115 (top); Jim Cumming/Shutterstock, 115 (bottom); Makarov Konstantin/Shutterstock, 117; Oliver Denker/Shutterstock, 123; Steve Gribben/JHUAPL/NASA/Wikimedia, 124; Aaron Taubm/USSF 30th Space Wing/KSC/NASA, 125; UCLA/PSI/MPS/DLR/IDA/JPL-Caltech/NASA, 126; Paris Musées/Science Source, 128; Giotto Project/ESA/JPL/NASA, 128–129; GSFC/NASA, 131, 135, 155, 158, 160, 161; David Ionut/Shutterstock, 133; UCLA/JPL-Caltech/NASA, 136; Tragoolchitr Jittasaiyapan/Shutterstock, 138 (top), 148; SSC/JPL-Caltech/NASA, 138 (bottom); GSFC/JPL-Caltech/NASA, 139; EHT/ESO, 143; Brian Donovan/Shutterstock, 146 (top); Derek Brumby/Shutterstock, 146 (bottom); David Ducros/ESA/Science Source, 152; Gaia/DPAC/ESA/Science Source, 153 (top); Hubble Collaboration and K. Noll STScI/AURA-ESA/NASA, 154; Hubble/ESA/GSFC/NASA, 163; Royal Astronomical Society/Science Source, 164; Kit Leong/Shutterstock, 165; CXC/STScI/UIUC/U of MN/JPL-Caltech/NASA, 166; Z. Levay and R. van der Marel/ STScI/ T. Hallas and A. Mellinger/ESA/GSFC/NASA, 168; Lynette Cook/Science Source, 169, 183; J. Lotz and the HFF Team/ESA/GSFC/NASA, 170; Yuri Zvezdny/Shutterstock, 172–173; ESA/Planck Collaboration/JPL/NASA, 176–177; E. Hallman/ESA/NASA, 179; E. Jullo/P. Natarajan/J-P. Kneib/ESA/GSFC/NASA, 180; SPL/Science Source, 181; Matt L. Photography/Shutterstock, 185; Chris Gunn/GSFC/NASA, 186

ABDOBOOKS.COM
Published by Abdo Publishing, a division of ABDO, PO Box 398166, Minneapolis, Minnesota 55439. Copyright © 2023 by Abdo Consulting Group, Inc. International copyrights reserved in all countries. No part of this book may be reproduced in any form without written permission from the publisher. Abdo Reference™ is a trademark and logo of Abdo Publishing.

Printed in the United States of America, North Mankato, Minnesota.
052022
092022

Editor: Arnold Ringstad
Series Designer: Colleen McLaren

LIBRARY OF CONGRESS CONTROL NUMBER: 2021952341

PUBLISHER'S CATALOGING-IN-PUBLICATION DATA
Names: Radley, Gail, author.
Title: The space encyclopedia / by Gail Radley
Description: Minneapolis, Minnesota: Abdo Publishing, 2023 | Series: Science encyclopedias | Includes online resources and index.
Identifiers: ISBN 9781532198762 (lib. bdg.) | ISBN 9781098272418 (ebook)
Subjects: LCSH: Outer space--Juvenile literature. | Cosmology--Juvenile literature. | Planets--Juvenile literature. | Solar system--Juvenile literature. | Astronomy--Juvenile literature. | Universe--Juvenile literature. | Encyclopedias and dictionaries--Juvenile literature.
Classification: DDC 523.1--dc23